CIPS STUDY MATTERS

CERTIFICATE IN
PROCUREMENT AND SUPPLY OPERATIONS

COURSE BOOK

Procurement and supply principles

Printed and distributed by:

The Chartered Institute of Purchasing & Supply, Easton House, Easton on the Hill, Stamford, Lincolnshire PE9 3NZ
Tel: +44 (0) 1780 756 777
Fax: +44 (0) 1780 751 610
Email: info@cips.org
Website: www.cips.org

First edition September 2012

Contents

Preface

Welcome to your new Course Book.

Your Course Book provides detailed coverage of all topics specified in the unit content.

For a full explanation of how to use your new Course Book, turn now to page ix. And good luck in your studies!

A note on style

Throughout your Course Book you will find that we use the masculine form of personal pronouns. This convention is adopted purely for the sake of stylistic convenience – we just don't like saying 'he/she' all the time. Please don't think this reflects any kind of bias or prejudice.

September 2012

The Unit Content

The unit content is reproduced below, together with reference to the chapter in this Course Book where each topic is covered.

At the start of every chapter in the Course Book we print an extract from the unit content below to indicate which areas of the unit content we will be covering in that chapter.

Unit purpose and aim(s)

On completion of the unit, candidates will be able to describe fundamental principles of procurement, supply and supply chains.

In any organisation, a significant proportion of costs are accounted for by the purchases of products, services or constructional works. Equally, any organisation will also be supplying products, services or works to their customers, whether these are other organisations, consumers or the public.

Learning outcomes, assessment criteria and indicative content

		Chapter
1.0	**Know the roles of procurement and supply within organisations**	
1.1	Define the common terms that describe aspects of procurement and supply	
	• Definitions of common terms such as procurement, purchasing, buying, supply chain, materials management, distribution, logistics and contract management	**1**
1.2	Describe the roles of procurement and supply in organisations	
	• The typical proportion of costs accounted for by procurements of goods and services	**2**
	• The roles of procurement and supply and procurement professionals	**2**
	• Achieving value for money	**2**
	• Sustainability in procurement and supply	**2**
	• The roles of staff with devolved responsibilities for procurement	**2**
1.3	Describe the benefits of effective procurement for organisations	
	• How effective procurement impacts on profitability – the profit contribution effect	**3**
	• Creating savings and improving efficiency	**3**
	• Budgets and budget monitoring	**3**
	• How effective procurement helps achieve targets	**3**
1.4	Identify the five rights of procurement and supply	
	• The five rights of procurement and supply	**4**
	• Price/total cost, quality, timing, quantity and place	**4**
	• Defining value for money	**4**

How to Use Your Course Book

Organising your study

'Organising' is the key word: unless you are a very exceptional student, you will find a haphazard approach is insufficient, particularly if you are having to combine study with the demands of a full-time job.

A good starting point is to timetable your studies, in broad terms, between now and the date of your assessment. How many subjects are you attempting? How many chapters are there in the Course Book for each subject? Now do the sums: how many days/weeks do you have for each chapter to be studied?

Remember:

- Not every week can be regarded as a study week – you may be going on holiday, for example, or there may be weeks when the demands of your job are particularly heavy. If these can be foreseen, you should allow for them in your timetabling.
- You also need a period leading up to the exam in which you will revise and practise what you have learned.

Once you have done the calculations, make a week-by-week timetable for yourself for each paper, allowing for study and revision of the entire unit content between now and the date of the assessment.

Getting started

Aim to find a quiet and undisturbed location for your study, and plan as far as possible to use the same period each day. Getting into a routine helps avoid wasting time. Make sure you have all the materials you need before you begin – keep interruptions to a minimum.

Using the Course Book

You should refer to the Course Book to the extent that you need it.

- If you are a newcomer to the subject, you will probably need to read through the Course Book quite thoroughly. This will be the case for most students.
- If some areas are already familiar to you – either through earlier studies or through your practical work experience – you may choose to skip sections of the Course Book.

The content of the Course Book

This Course Book has been designed to give detailed coverage of every topic in the unit content. As you will see from pages vii–viii, each topic mentioned in the unit content is dealt with in a chapter of the Course Book. For the most part the order of the Course Book follows the order of the unit content closely, though departures from this principle have occasionally been made in the interest of a logical learning order.

Each chapter begins with a reference to the assessment criteria and indicative content to be covered in the chapter. Each chapter is divided into sections, listed in the introduction to the chapter, and for the most part being actual captions from the unit content.

All of this enables you to monitor your progress through the unit content very easily and provides reassurance that you are tackling every subject that is assessable.

Each chapter contains the following features.

- Clear coverage of each topic in a concise and approachable format
- A chapter summary
- Self-test questions

The study phase

For each chapter you should begin by glancing at the main headings (listed at the start of the chapter). Then read fairly rapidly through the body of the text to absorb the main points. If it's there in the text, you can be sure it's there for a reason, so try not to skip unless the topic is one you are familiar with already.

Then return to the beginning of the chapter to start a more careful reading. You may want to take brief notes as you go along.

Test your recall and understanding of the material by attempting the self-test questions. These are accompanied by cross-references to paragraphs where you can check your answers and refresh your memory.

The revision phase

Your approach to revision should be methodical and you should aim to tackle each main area of the unit content in turn. Re-read your notes. Then do some question practice. The CIPS website contains many past exam questions and you should aim to identify those that are suitable for the unit you are studying.

Additional reading

Your Course Book provides you with the key information needed for each module but CIPS strongly advocates reading as widely as possible to augment and reinforce your understanding. CIPS produces an official reading list of books, which can be downloaded from the bookshop area of the CIPS website.

To help you, we have identified one essential textbook for each subject. We recommend that you read this for additional information.

The essential textbook for this unit is *Purchasing and Supply Chain Management* by Kenneth Lysons and Brian Farrington.

CHAPTER 1

Aspects of Procurement and Supply

Assessment criteria and indicative content

1.1 Define the common terms that describe aspects of procurement and supply

- Definitions of common terms such as procurement, purchasing, buying, supply chain, materials management, distribution, logistics and contract management

Section headings

1 Procurement, purchasing and buying
2 Supply chains
3 Materials management, distribution and logistics
4 Contract management
5 Purchasing in service organisations

1 Procurement, purchasing and buying

Introduction to purchasing and procurement

1.1 Every organisation has some involvement with purchasing. This may range from a very low level – perhaps the maintenance of stock in a stationery cupboard – right through to organisations in which purchasing represents the very life-blood of the business – perhaps the manufacture of motor cars. All of these organisations have one thing in common: they are all striving to satisfy the needs of an end user, the person who buys or uses the goods or services that the organisation provides.

1.2 The people who carry out such purchasing activities are required to spend their organisations' funds carefully and wisely. To do this, they can benefit from a study of the principles and practice underlying the purchasing profession. Our objective in this Course Book is to provide an introduction to these principles and to describe the best practice observed by professional purchasers.

1.3 To begin, we use this first chapter to define and explain some common terms that you will come across again and again throughout your studies. We begin with the concepts of procurement, purchasing and buying.

The meaning of purchasing

1.4 Doesn't everyone know the meaning of purchasing? We all do it every day: purchasing food, newspapers, clothes, petrol, life assurance, transport services and a thousand other things.

What's more, many readers of this Course Book will already be doing it in a professional capacity in the course of their jobs: purchasing materials, components, services and other requirements for the organisation that employs them.

1.5 All this may be true – but it skims over an important point. There is a big difference between doing something in everyday life and doing it as a professional. And there is even a difference between doing something as a professional and understanding it in the way that professional education requires.

1.6 Organisational purchasing is a professional discipline based on a foundation of study and research, and proceeding according to systematic guidelines on best practice. To do well in your purchasing exams, it will not be sufficient to have a general awareness of what purchasing is – or even what purchasing involves in your own day-to-day work. You must be prepared to look critically and in depth at the conceptual and best practice foundations of the subject.

1.7 Purchasing for organisations is clearly different from the kind of purchasing we do for our own personal purposes. When buying food, newspapers and other items, we do not go through the same rigorous decision-making procedures as we would to buy a component for use in our firm's manufacturing activities, or stock for our firm's retail activities. Why not? Because organisational buying is simply different from our own (consumer) buying.

1.8 In simple terms, **organisational buying** involves the following activities.

- The use of resources which belong to the owners (or shareholders) of the organisation. Buyers are accountable to the owners, and those who manage the organisation on their behalf, for the efficient and effective use of resources: they can't simply spend or risk them according to their own whims, as we can do in our personal spending.
- The acquisition of items that will satisfy the requirements of other people and be suitable inputs for defined processes and systems. Buyers must purchase the right items for these people, processes and systems: they can't simply choose items according to their own preferences. The people who actually use the items and services obtained by buyers are often referred to as **users** or **user departments**. For example, purchasing may obtain computer hardware for use by the finance department; in this case, the finance department is the user.
- Working together with others in a complex network of relationships, work flows and accountabilities. Buyers must adhere to schedules, budgets, policies, plans and procedures, in order for their work to be properly co-ordinated with the general flow of work in and through the organisation: they can't simply make decisions by their own criteria, in their own time, in their own way.
- Developing and maintaining constructive working relations with suppliers who provide the items the organisation needs. Buyers must consider the impact of their decisions and actions (a) on suppliers' ability to fulfil their part of the purchase contract effectively and (b) on suppliers' motivation and commitment to ongoing relationship.

1.9 In other words, purchasing is a discipline. It operates according to a framework of principle and best practice, designed to help purchasers to fulfil their role in a properly responsible, professional, effective and efficient way.

- *Responsible*: purchasers are accountable for their decisions, and they make those decisions rationally, ethically, and in the best interests of the organisation.
- *Professional*: purchasers reflect and uphold the educational, technical and ethical standards of the purchasing profession.

- *Effective*: purchasers achieve the objectives set for their work, implementing purchasing plans and projects successfully.
- *Efficient*: purchasers achieve their objectives with the least possible waste of resources – money, physical resources, time and effort.

1.10 Let's start with some general models of what purchasing is about, to give us an overview.

What is purchasing for?

1.11 Most obviously, the general objective of purchasing is to obtain or source the 'supplies' or 'inputs' required by an organisation. The term 'inputs' means the resources that the organisation employs or buys from suppliers in order to carry out its activities. (The term 'outputs' means the products or services produced by the organisation for its customers.)

1.12 As we will see in more detail a bit later, different types of organisation will require different types of inputs: a manufacturing organisation may require raw materials or components to make into products; a retail organisation may require finished goods to sell on to consumers; while a service organisation may require equipment, information and people to provide services to customers. But the principle is the same in each case.

1.13 The organisation can be seen as an **open system** which takes in inputs from the environment (including those obtained by the purchasing function on its behalf) and processes them in some way to create outputs to the environment: Figure 1.1.

Figure 1.1 *The organisation as an open system*

1.14 The primary task of purchasing is therefore to provide the 'right' inputs for the organisation's processes. The 'right' inputs are traditionally described as:

- Inputs of the right quality
- Delivered in the right quantity
- To the right place
- At the right time
- For the right price.

These are often called the five rights of purchasing, and we will discuss them in more detail in Chapter 4.

Procurement

1.15 The terminology relating to purchasing can be somewhat vague. Many people use terms such as buying, purchasing and procurement interchangeably. And in many contexts this doesn't matter

– the meaning intended will usually be quite clear. However, some authorities have attempted to distinguish between the terms.

- **Purchasing** is defined as 'buying or obtaining goods or services which are paid for'. (This implies that purchasing is a slightly broader concept than buying.)
- **Procurement** is defined as 'obtaining goods or services in any way including hiring, leasing, borrowing or stealing'.

1.16 Clearly procurement is a more general term than purchasing. It is usually taken to embrace activities prior to the establishment of a purchase contract. For example, it includes identification of a need, and sourcing (ie identifying and evaluating potential suppliers). It also includes such post-contract activities as contract management and management of supplier relations. On this analysis, purchasing is just one aspect of the wider procurement function, and includes activities such as ordering, expediting, receipt of goods into stock, and payments to suppliers. Don't worry if some of these terms are unfamiliar to you – we will be returning to them later in the Course Book.

2 Supply chains

What is a supply chain?

2.1 We said earlier that an organisation will try to satisfy the needs of an end user – the customer who wants to buy the organisation's products or services. However, it is rare for one organisation to satisfy the needs of an end user on its own because the process – which may start with the production of raw materials and end with an over-the-counter sale in a retail shop – is too complex for any single organisation to cope with.

2.2 As a result, there are likely to be other organisations which are directly involved with specific aspects of the process. When we consider all of these organisations together we call them a 'supply chain'. The supply chain and each of its elements is dedicated to meeting the needs of the end user although some of them may have no direct contact with that end-user.

2.3 In a general sense, 'supply' may be defined simply as the act (or process) of providing something or making something available, often in response to buyers' or customers' requirements. It involves the transfer or flow of goods, services and information from one party to another.

2.4 The concept of the 'supply chain' can therefore be defined as follows.

- 'The supply chain includes all those involved in organising and converting materials through the input stages (raw materials), conversion phase (work in progress) and outputs (finished products) The cycle is often repeated several times in the journey from the individual producer to the ultimate customer, as one organisation's finished good is another's input.' *(Baily et al)*
- A supply chain is 'that network of organisations that are involved, through upstream and downstream linkages, in the different processes and activities that produce value in the form of products and services in the hands of the ultimate customer.' *(Christopher)*
- 'The supply chain encompasses all organisations and activities associated with the flow and transformation of goods from the raw materials stage, through to the end user, as well as the associated information flows. Material and information flow both up and down the supply chain.' *(Handfield & Nichols)*

2.5 The principal flows in a very simple supply chain are shown in Figure 1.2. In fact, as highlighted by Handfield and Nichols, it is not quite this simple: there are multiple, two-way flows along the chain. Information (in the form of enquiries, specifications, orders and delivery schedules) flows from customers *backwards* to suppliers. Then products and services (or the fulfilment of orders) flow forward through the chain, as shown in our diagram. More information (confirming receipt of the order or giving feedback) and payment then flow back again.

2.6 Nevertheless, we can think of the basic 'stream' as flowing from a first supplier (perhaps a raw material extractor) to a final consumer, so in relation to the firm we are focusing on (the 'focal firm'):

- Suppliers (the firms from which it *buys* the *inputs* to its activities) are said to be **upstream**; and
- Customers (the firms or individuals to whom it *sells* the *outputs* of its activities) are said to be **downstream**.

Figure 1.2 *Principal flows in a simple supply chain*

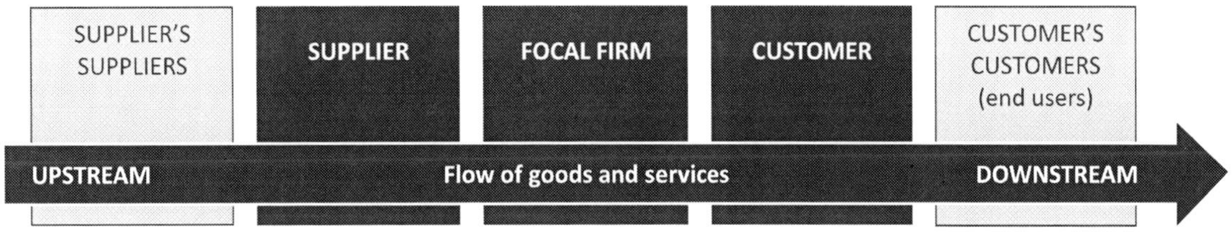

2.7 It is important for the purposes of this unit to remember that a focal firm is both a purchasing organisation (dealing with suppliers to acquire inputs to its activities) and a selling organisation (dealing with customers to sell the outputs of its activities).

- The firm's **upstream activities** (the supply chain seen from the focal firm's perspective as a purchasing organisation) therefore include processes such as search, procurement, usage, maintenance and disposal of goods and services – and the management of relationships with suppliers.
- The firm's **downstream activities** (the supply chain seen from the focal firm's perspective as a selling organisation) include processes such as research, design, manufacture, selling and servicing of goods and services – and the management of relationships with customers.

Why think of supply as a 'chain'?

2.8 Commercial relationships – like interpersonal relationships – require at least two parties who are in contact with each other. Much of the effort of purchasing professionals, as we will see, is devoted to supplier selection, development, performance management and relationship management; and the development of strategic relationships (such as partnerships and alliances) with selected suppliers of the most important goods and services.

2.9 However, these kinds of focused supplier-customer exchanges usually happen within the context of a lengthier supply process. An extractor or producer of raw materials supplies to a processing plant or producer of components, which supplies to a manufacturing or assembly organisation, which supplies to a distributor or retail outlet, which supplies to the consumer. It is this total configuration which is often called a chain, or channel. (You may like to consider what parties and processes the supply chain would consist of, for a range of different products and services: the sort of exam question that may come up on this area of the syllabus.)

2.10 The chain metaphor highlights several useful characteristics of the supply process and relationships.

- It emphasises 'serial co-operation' or 'working together in turn': each player contributes value at its stage of the sequence of activities.
- It emphasises mutual dependency and collaboration, because each link in a chain is essential to the completeness and strength of the whole: weak links and breakages (eg an underperforming or failing supplier or distributor) may disrupt the flow of supply.
- It emphasises 'linkages' between members: value is added not just by each element in the chain, but by the quality of the relationships between them.

2.11 We will be looking at the supply chain concept in more detail in the final chapter of this Course Book.

3 Materials management, distribution and logistics

Introduction

3.1 As we have already seen, the process of obtaining inputs is increasingly considered in relation to 'supply chains': as an issue of developing and managing flows of goods and value towards an end customer – not just as a series of one-to-one transactions or contractual relationships.

3.2 Procurement specialists now commonly take responsibility for many matters which go beyond the traditional activities of buying and contract administration. In particular, a more holistic view of the supply chain has emphasised the need to break down functional boundaries and barriers, so that materials-related activities can be *integrated* within a single management framework.

3.3 The terms 'function', 'functional', 'cross-functional' etc often confuse newcomers to the subject. 'Function' can mean a department (so the purchasing function can mean the staff who carry out purchasing activities). Equally, it can mean the activities carried out within a department (so the purchasing function may refer to all the activities performed by purchasing staff). 'Cross-functional' refers to situations when more than one department may be involved in an activity or project.

3.4 Dividing responsibility for inbound flows of materials between different functions, such as purchasing, transport, stores and production has historically led to difficulties in co-ordination, and also meant that no single manager took responsibility for total materials costs. This resulted in a lack of 'big picture' and 'joined up' thinking about how materials flows could be improved or streamlined to add value.

3.5 The attempt to achieve integration, cross-functional collaboration and joined-up thinking has formed a major trend in process organisation in recent decades. There has been progressive integration of materials activities, towards a 'total integration' picture which is often given the name 'logistics': Figure 1.3.

Figure 1.3 *Integration of supply chain activities*

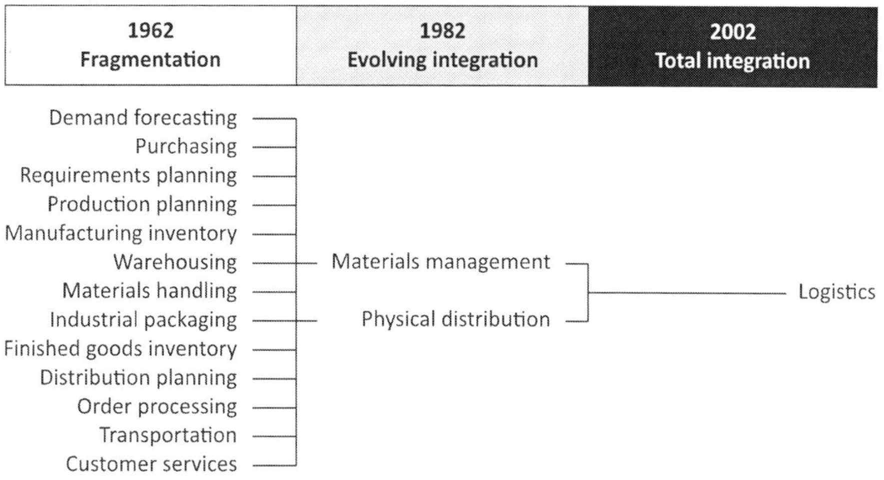

Adapted from *The Management of Business Logistics*, by Coyle, Bardi and Langley

Materials management

3.6 Materials management (MM) has been defined as 'the total of all those tasks, functions, activities and routines which concern the transfer of external materials and services into the organisation and the administration of the same until they are consumed or used in the process of production, operations or sales' (CIPS).

3.7 The CIPS definition emphasises that materials management involves activities in the *input phase* of the supply chain process: that is, the flow of goods into production., through sourcing and purchasing, inbound transport, storage of materials and delivery to their point of use.

3.8 Materials management may therefore include key activities such as the following.

- Materials and inventory planning: eg budgeting, product research and development, materials specifications and planning quantities to be purchased
- Procurement of the necessary materials, parts and supplies: processing requisitions; supply market research; sourcing; negotiation and contract award; the purchase to pay (P2P) cycle; contract and supplier management; and contracting for and supervising transport services for incoming items
- Storage and inventory management: stores or warehouse location and design; goods inwards (receiving and inspection) procedures; materials handling (unloading, moving, packaging and storing supplies); physical protection and control of stocks; issuing goods from stores to production; maintaining cost and inventory data; and disposing of surplus, obsolete or scrap items
- Production control: eg forward ordering of inputs; production scheduling; and quality management.

3.9 The advantages of co-ordinating materials-related activities in a single management framework can be summarised as follows.

- Costs relating to materials flows are isolated, enabling the materials manager to identify areas where costs are a concern and to take remedial action.
- Cost reductions may be achieved by eliminating wastes across the process.
- Cross-functional co-operation and co-ordination are improved by shared goals and management, emphasising a 'horizontal' flow of materials and information (rather than separate 'silos' of responsibility).

- Conflicting objectives can be reconciled, or trade-offs made in the best interests of the process as a whole. For example, purchasing's goal of achieving economies of scale might conflict with the stores department's goal of minimising inventory: a materials manager has the perspective to achieve the best balance between both objectives.

Physical distribution

3.10 Physical distribution involves activities involved in the *output phase* of the supply chain process: that is, the flow of goods *from* production to the customer: storage and handling of finished outputs, and outbound transport to intermediaries, customers or consumers.

3.11 Physical distribution management (PDM) is the method by which the outputs of production are moved from one location to another: typically, from a supplier to a customer. This involves the traditional combining of:

- Warehousing and storage
- Transport or distribution planning: optimising freight loads, transport routes and delivery schedules for cost-efficient (and environmentally sustainable) delivery
- Materials handling (eg moving, loading, packaging or containerising for outbound transport)
- Inventory management and control: keeping track of finished items in stock
- Transportation and delivery.

3.12 The basic objective of physical distribution is to deliver the right goods to the right place at the right time and at the right cost.

3.13 Physical distribution can be local, national or international: even 'global' or worldwide – which presents particular challenges of transport planning and risk management.

Logistics

3.14 The concept of logistics management takes integration a step further, by integrating responsibilities for both the *input phase and the output phase:* the flow of materials inwards to the production process *and* the flow of finished goods outwards to the customer.

3.15 Logistics management has been defined as: 'the process of planning, implementing and controlling the efficient, effective flow and storage of raw materials, in-process inventory, finished goods, services, and related information from point of origin to point of consumption... for the purpose of conforming to customer requirements' (Council of Logistics Management Professionals, USA, cited by Coyle, Bardi and Langley, *The Management of Business Logistics*).

3.16 In other words, logistics potentially embraces the full range of supply chain activity, with an emphasis on the effective and efficient satisfaction of end-customer requirements.

4 Contract management

Contracts

4.1 The role of a contract is to set out the roles, rights and obligations of both parties in a transaction or relationship. A contract implies an intention to 'enter into legal relations': that is, both parties agree to be legally bound by the specified roles and responsibilities. It may take the form of a spoken agreement or 'understanding' (eg based on a regular trading relationship that has developed over time), but more complex contracts are usually formalised in writing.

4.2 Contract law is a highly complex area, beyond the scope of this syllabus: you will study it in detail later in your purchasing studies. However, you should be aware of the nature of a purchase contract, as a statement of:

- Exactly what two or more parties have agreed to do or exchange (specifications, prices, delivery and payment dates and so on)
- Conditions and contingencies which may alter the arrangement (eg circumstances under which it would not be reasonable to enforce certain terms, or agreement that if Party A does x, then Party B may do y)
- The rights of each party if the other fails to do what it has agreed to do ('remedies' for 'breach of contract')
- How responsibility or 'liability' will be apportioned in the event of problems (eg who pays for damage to or loss of goods)
- How any disputes will be resolved (eg by arbitration).

4.3 Once contracts are signed it is not as simple as saying: 'The supplier will now do *that.*' There will be obligations to be followed up on either side. If contingencies arise, the contract may (or may not) lay down what happens next. If the supplier's performance falls short in any way, there will be a variety of options for pursuing the dispute, enforcing the terms of the contract or gaining remedies (such as compensation). Circumstances and requirements may change, and contract terms may have to be adjusted accordingly. This is an ongoing process through the life of the contract – which is where contract management comes in.

What is contract management?

4.4 Contract management is a process designed to ensure that both parties to a contract meet their obligations, and that the intended outcomes of a contract are delivered. As we have already suggested, it also involves building a good working relationship between the buyer and supplier, continuing through the life of a contract.

4.5 The key processes and activities involved in contract management are described in Table 1.1.

Table 1.1 *Key elements of contract management*

ELEMENT	COMMENTS
Contract development	The formulation of a legally binding agreement, setting out detailed terms and conditions of business, and the specification of requirement.
Contract manager (or contract management team)	For smaller contracts, a single individual may be able to carry out all contract management responsibilities, but for larger contracts, a team may be required, especially in the early stages, which are often more demanding in terms of management time.
Contract administration	Contract administration is concerned with the implementation of procedures, by buyer and supplier, to ensure that contract obligations are fulfilled.
Managing contract performance	Service level agreements (SLAs) and performance measures may be developed to express the desired outputs from the contract: these documents will form an operational tool with which the respective contract managers can monitor performance on a day-to-day basis. Such documentation will usually be more flexible than the contract document itself.
Relationship management	Developing the working relationship between the purchaser and supplier, through regular contacts, communication and information-sharing; developing and applying supplier incentives; managing and resolving conflicts; developing approaches to collaboration and mutual support; and so on.
Contract renewal or termination	Towards the end of the contract period, the buyer's contract manager should review both the success of the contract and the relationship and the status of the supply need. If an ongoing need remains, and the contract has been satisfactorily fulfilled, it may be renewed. If the need has been met, or performance has been unsatisfactory, it may be terminated.

The role of the contract manager

4.6 The main responsibilities of a contract manager (or contract management team) on the buyer's side are as follows.

- To act as a single point of contact for all commercial and legal correspondence relating to the contract
- To maintain the specification of contract performance measures
- To monitor contract performance and report on overall service levels
- To represent the buyer's interest to the supplier
- To oversee operation and administration of the contract
- To determine and take remedial actions, in agreement with the supplier, on any problems that arise
- To negotiate remedies with the supplier, in the event of breach of contract terms
- To escalate contract disputes to higher levels, if necessary
- To maintain revised and updated contract specifications
- To advise and support operational managers in other functions, to whom day-to-day management and monitoring of contracts which affect them may be devolved. (For example, purchasing may hand over management of a contract to install IT systems to the IT manager, or managers of user departments.)

4.7 The main responsibilities of the contract manager on the supplier side are as follows.

- To monitor contract performance
- To identify and manage exceptions (cases where things have gone wrong)
- To represent the supplier's interests to the buyer

- To respond to changing customer needs
- To determine and take remedial actions, in agreement with the buyer, on any problems that arise
- To negotiate remedies with the buyer, in the event of a breach of contract
- To escalate contract disputes to higher levels, if necessary
- To operate and administer the contract to the specification

4.8 Like an account manager in a marketing department, an effective contract manager requires a range of project management, administrative, decision-making, problem-solving and interpersonal skills (communicating, negotiating, managing conflict). He or she also requires detailed knowledge of contract development, performance specification and measurement, budgeting, purchasing – and the organisation's particular policies, procedures, systems and documents for each of these tasks.

Benefits of effective contract management

4.9 Many of the cost savings and improvements available from supplier management are achieved by how buyer and supplier work together *after* the contract has been awarded. If contracts are not well managed by the buying organisation the following adverse outcomes may occur.

- The supplier may be obliged to take control of contract performance and problem-solving, resulting in unbalanced decisions that do not serve the purchaser's interests.
- Decisions may not be taken at the right time (or at all).
- Buyer and supplier may fail to understand – and fulfil – their obligations and responsibilities.
- There may be misunderstandings and disagreements, and too many issues may be escalated inappropriately, damaging the relationship.
- Progress may be slow, or there may be an inability to move forward.
- The intended benefits from the contract may not be realised.
- Opportunities to improve value for money and performance may be missed.

4.10 On the other hand, the benefits of positive contract management include: improved risk management in developing and managing contracts; improved compliance and commitment by the supplier; incentives and momentum for ongoing relationship and performance improvement; and better value for money (arising from efficient contract administration and performance).

5 Purchasing in service organisations

The importance of the services sector

5.1 A major force in increasing the strategic role of purchasing functions has been the development of manufacturing operations. It is in the manufacturing sector that purchasing was first practised as a professional discipline, and it is still probably true to say that this is the sector in which the function is most fully developed. Much of the purchasing literature (including this Course Book) is based primarily on purchasing practice in the manufacturing sector. We take the opportunity here to emphasise that purchasing disciplines are becoming increasingly important in service organisations also.

5.2 In developed economies, recent decades have seen dramatic growth in the services sector: banking and insurance, legal and accountancy services, advertising, consultancy, catering, cleaning, education and training and a host of others. Organisations such as these are not providing a tangible product (or if they are, it is only an incidental part of their main 'offering' – like the course handouts that might be included in a staff training course).

5.3 In many service companies the purchasing function is relatively undeveloped. Indeed, it is sometimes found that many purchasing responsibilities are undertaken by non-purchasing personnel because a centralised purchasing function is either completely absent or ineffective.

5.4 This is an area which is both a concern and an opportunity for the purchasing profession. It is a concern because service companies account for a huge share of gross domestic product and purchasing disciplines should not be neglected. It is an opportunity because many such companies are at present failing to realise benefits which a strong purchasing input could bring.

5.5 Generalisations are always dangerous, but it is probably fair to say that in many service companies purchasing activities are dispersed throughout the organisation, rather than being under centralised control; and if a centralised function exists at all, its role is mainly clerical and administrative. This situation is changing as increased competition forces service companies to examine value added throughout their supply chains, but the stage of development is less advanced than in manufacturing organisations.

5.6 One characteristic that has held back the development of purchasing functions in service companies is the absence of a clear link between inputs, processing and outputs. In the case of a manufacturing company this link is very clear: materials are bought in for $X, these are worked on at a cost of $Y and eventually converted into finished products for sale at $Z.

5.7 In a service company this process is much less clear, especially since the value of bought in materials is usually low as a percentage of sales output. For example, whereas a manufacturer might expect, say, 60 per cent of his sales revenue to be absorbed by the cost of materials purchased from outside suppliers, for a service company the proportion might be as low as 10 per cent. Most of the inputs of many service companies consist of staff salaries, where purchasing expertise has little to contribute.

5.8 What items are bought from outside in a typical service organisation? This will obviously depend heavily on the exact nature of the organisation, but the following are likely answers.

- Office equipment and supplies such as stationery
- Computer hardware and software
- Motor vehicles
- Advertising and design services
- Maintenance services (for computers, vehicles and buildings)
- In some cases, capital goods (such as a provider of logistics services who must invest heavily in premises, materials handling equipment, heavy goods vehicles etc)

5.9 In a manufacturing company a purchasing manager's main 'customer' is the production function. In a service company hardly any of the buyer's effort is directed at 'production'. This is well illustrated by the list above. For this reason among others line managers in such companies have tended to think of purchasing purely as a support function and this has been a factor in the low priority given to purchasing expertise.

Modern trends in the services sector

5.10 However, a number of trends are beginning to alter this picture. One is the increased use of **outsourcing**. As service companies focus on core activities they are increasingly likely to outsource such support functions as security, catering, printing, and information technology. The logical conclusion to this development is the use of a facilities management approach under which all such activities are placed under the responsibility of a single facilities manager. We return to this topic in Chapter 6.

5.11 Another trend with important implications for purchasing is the increased size of service companies and the increased scale of their operations, often resulting from mergers and takeovers which reduce the number of companies operating in any particular sector. Once operations have reached a certain scale the desirability of defined purchasing responsibilities becomes more pressing.

5.12 This is clearer in companies where capital spending is relatively high. Because large sums of money are involved, the impetus to adopt appropriate purchasing techniques may well be present. Without this, the purchase of specialist capital equipment (eg computer hardware and systems) may be left to users whose priorities are not mainly directed to low cost. From their perspective, reliability and quality are vital, value for money less so.

5.13 More generally, it can be said that when responsibility for purchasing decisions is spread throughout an organisation, management lose the important 'value for money' perspective. End users of the items purchased are not trained to emphasise this criterion and may instead focus on a solution which has worked reliably in the past, without considering whether better or lower-cost solutions may now be available.

5.14 In all these instances the value of a strong purchasing function is clear. If purchasing expertise is directed only at routine low-cost items the scope for cost efficiencies is much reduced. By extending the scope of purchasing involvement senior managers can obtain cost benefits that may be vital in securing competitive advantage.

5.15 This sounds easy enough, but in practice difficulties are encountered. The first hurdle to overcome is at the level of senior managers. Unless they can be persuaded of the strategic importance of the issue any initiative from the purchasing department is likely to fail.

5.16 Even with the support of senior management, there are obstacles that must be removed. Chief among these is the probable reluctance of operational managers to hand over purchasing responsibility. They may perceive purchasing staff as having different priorities from themselves, and may resist what they see as merely a cost cutting exercise. Purchasing must be able to convince them that, while cost is important, operational priorities (such as reliability and delivery lead time) will also be addressed with no less enthusiasm than in the past.

Service supply chains

5.17 In service organisations, the value of bought-in materials is generally a low proportion of sales output and total input: such organisations are highly labour-intensive. However, physical supply may be important if services are based on the use of physical or 'hard' assets: property (as in a hotel or bank branch), vehicles (as in a logistics company or airline) or machinery (as in a computer bureau or printing service). In addition, service organisations commonly buy in goods and services for their own use: office equipment and supplies, computer systems, vehicles, advertising and design services, maintenance services and so on.

5.18 Various trends can be observed in service supply chains.

- Services are increasingly about the management and supply of information: financial services, information and research, entertainment and transport bookings, consultancy, advertising and design and so on. Many information storage, query and processing functions have been automated – and can now be offered direct to the consumer through the internet, interactive kiosks, ATM machines and so on. Supply chains are thus shortening to direct interaction between the service provider and consumer, increasingly on a self-service basis.

- Information can replace inventory (eg in the case of Dell's assembled-to-order computers).
- Services are increasingly outsourced, as organisations focus on core activities and subcontract support functions such as security, catering, printing, IT, sales and customer service, fleet management, HR selection and training, logistics and facilities management.
- The combination of automation and outsourcing has enabled the development of virtual service organisations and networks. Financial services are a good example: mortgages, insurance and investment products are often supplied by a network of providers, drawn on by brokers who interface with consumers.

5.19 Perhaps the key point about service supply chains is the importance of people in delivering service and differentiating one service provider from another. Training, motivation, empowerment and cultural values are important factors in service supply. Supply chain management will also contribute to competitive advantage through cost efficiency and the integrated management of information.

Chapter summary

- Organisational buying is a professional discipline that involves more structured and formalised procedures than consumer buying.
- The supply chain concept recognises that a number of interlinked organisations are typically involved in delivering value to an ultimate consumer. Buyers must manage the whole supply chain, not just their own organisation.
- The term 'logistics' incorporates both upstream activities (managing suppliers and their suppliers) and downstream activities (delivering value to our own customers and their customers).
- Buyers usually establish legal contracts with suppliers. Once a contract is awarded, the buyer still has work to do in ensuring that the contract is fulfilled and delivers the outcomes required.
- Much of the purchasing literature focuses on the manufacturing sector, but nowadays (in developed economies) purchasing disciplines are increasingly found also in service organisations.

Self-test questions

Numbers in brackets refer to the paragraphs where you can check your answers.

1 What activities are involved in the process of organisational buying? (1.8)

2 What does it mean to say that an organisation is an 'open system'? (1.13)

3 Define 'supply chain'. (2.4)

4 What is meant by upstream and downstream activities? (2.6)

5 What aspects of the supply process are captured by the supply chain metaphor? (2.10)

6 Define 'materials management'. (3.6)

7 What activities are involved in physical distribution management? (3.11)

8 What is contract management? (4.4)

9 List the main responsibilities of a contract manager on the buyer's side. (4.6)

10 List some examples of service businesses. (5.2)

11 What types of input are typically purchased by a service business? (5.8)

CHAPTER 2

The Roles of Procurement and Supply

Assessment criteria and indicative content

1.2 Describe the roles of procurement and supply in organisations

- The typical proportion of costs accounted for by procurements of goods and services
- The roles of procurement and supply and procurement professionals
- Achieving value for money
- Sustainability in procurement and supply
- The roles of staff with devolved responsibilities for procurement

Section headings

1 The scope of procurement
2 Procurement and supply professionals
3 Achieving value for money
4 Sustainability in procurement and supply
5 Staff with devolved responsibilities

1 The scope of procurement

The proportion of costs accounted for by procurement

1.1 An important trend in recent years has been a transformation of many organisations' cost bases. This applies particularly to manufacturing organisations, but other sectors have seen a similar change.

1.2 In years gone by, the largest expense borne by a typical manufacturer, by far, was the cost of wages. Most manufacturing industry was heavily labour intensive; most manufacturing processes were carried out manually by skilled and unskilled workers. The result was a large workforce and a large wages bill. In this area of (internal) expenditure of course purchasing staff had little or no role to play.

1.3 Today the situation is very different. Many industries have seen a huge investment in automated production processes. In many cases this has been accompanied by painful cuts in manufacturing personnel. From being labour intensive, such industries have become capital intensive. The sums invested in plant and equipment, often computer controlled, are high in relation to the sums paid out to employees.

1.4 A related trend is a new focus on core activities. Many businesses now see advantage in concentrating on certain core activities where they believe they hold competitive advantage.

Many support activities, which previously would have been provided by in-house departments, are now outsourced – handed over to specialist external suppliers who provide the required service in exchange for a fee. In some cases this trend has been accentuated by regulatory pressures. For example, in many public sector organisations a regime of market testing and compulsory competitive tendering has been imposed. This means that a public sector body is usually obliged to investigate possible external suppliers and to seek quotations from them to provide the required service.

1.5 This trend applies not just to the provision of services. Manufacturing businesses too have been increasingly ready to focus on just one part of the manufacturing process. Where previously they might have made Product X entirely from scratch, nowadays they buy the parts for Product X externally and restrict their own activities to the assembly process. Another organisation in the supply chain specialises in manufacturing the parts required for Product X.

1.6 Both of these trends point to the same outcome: organisations spend a much greater proportion of their income on buying in goods and services than they used to (external spending). The impact for purchasing departments is obvious. Where previously the purchasing responsibility extended only to a small proportion of the organisation's total spending, the proportion has now risen dramatically.

The financial impact of purchasing

1.7 Crucially, the financial impact of purchasing effectiveness and efficiency is a very direct one. Every dollar saved by purchasing activities is a dollar added to bottom line profit. On the other hand every dollar wasted by purchasing is a dollar lost to profit. Contrast this with the efforts of, say, a selling department, where every $1.00 gained in extra sales brings with it perhaps $0.90 of extra costs; the net impact on profit in that case is only a $0.10 boost.

1.8 This is not to say that selling departments are in any sense less important than purchasing departments. The purpose is merely to explain why the attention of senior managers has increasingly focused on the effective management of purchasing activities. This has been part of the reason for the increased status accorded to the purchasing function in recent years.

1.9 These ideas can be illustrated in a number of ways. One approach is to show the total organisational revenue as a 'cake' which has to be sliced up: one portion to pay external costs, one to pay internal costs (such as wages), and one (usually small!) slice left over for profit. For a typical manufacturing business the cake might be divided as shown in Figure 2.1.

Figure 2.1 *How income is spent*

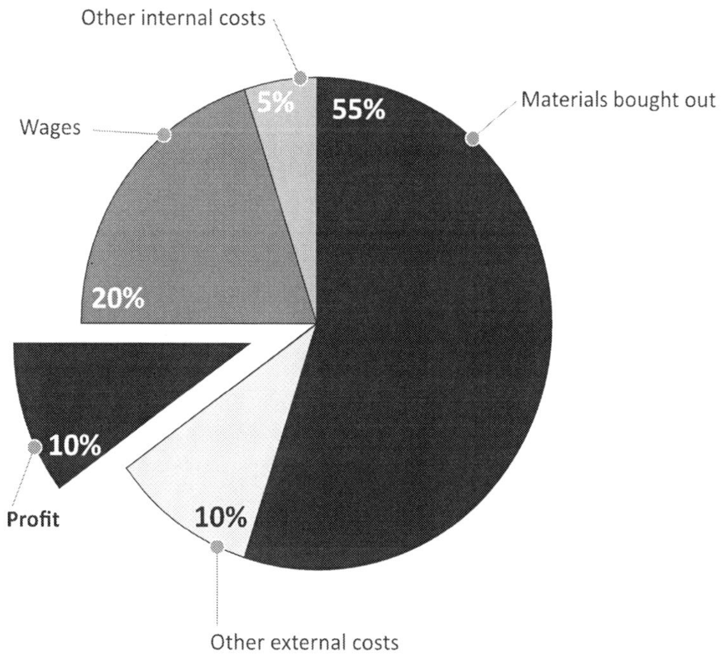

1.10 It should be easy to see from this that external costs typically consume a large part of the cake, and that if they are not controlled they could easily expand to eliminate the thin slice left for profit.

1.11 Another way of illustrating the impact of purchasing on organisational profitability is to compute some figures. Suppose that annual sales are $50m, with materials costs equal to 60 per cent of sales and 'internal' costs of $15m. Profit is therefore $5m (50 – 30 – 15 = $5m). Now look what happens if:

(a) sales volumes rise by 5%; or alternatively
(b) materials costs fall by 5%.

	(a)		*(b)*	
	$m	*$m*	*$m*	*$m*
Sales		52.5		50.0
Materials costs	31.5		28.5	
Internal costs	15.0		15.0	
Total costs		46.5		43.5
Net profit		6.0		6.5

1.12 The profit increase achieved by increasing sales volume is not as great as that achieved by reducing costs. (A 5% saving in costs has led to a 30% increase in profit, from $5m to $6.5m.) And the example does not even mention the other saving achieved by alternative (b): if materials costs are lower, then so too is the cost of inventory. A lower inventory value saves costs, and this saving ought to be added to the benefits already apparent from the figures above.

1.13 This discussion has been concerned only with the basic purchase price of supplies. The role of purchasing becomes even more important when we consider the wider concept of total acquisition cost or total cost of ownership: this is discussed later in this Course Book.

2 Procurement and supply professionals

Historical development of the role

2.1 It used to be a simple matter to define the work performed by purchasing staff. This was because the purchasing function used to be regarded as a reactive support service, responding to the needs of other functions as they arose by performing routine clerical and administrative tasks.

2.2 This outlook has changed radically over the years. The view of the purchasing function is now typically more strategic in nature. The range of tasks to be completed is broader and the complexity of the purchasing operations is greater. However, it is still possible to distinguish a number of broad areas of responsibility.

2.3 Clerical and administrative tasks remain vital even in a more strategic environment. Record keeping, origination and processing of purchase orders and other documentation, and storage and retrieval of data are essential to the smooth running of the department. These tasks are usually to a greater or lesser degree automated and the amount of man hours expended on such activities is a declining proportion of overall purchasing effort.

2.4 Negotiating and buying are perhaps the core activities of a purchasing function. This category of work includes locating, assessing and selecting potential suppliers, as well as settling terms and conditions between buyer and seller.

2.5 Expediting (ie chasing suppliers to ensure they deliver on time) is another typical purchasing activity. Like other non-value adding activities, expediting is increasingly tackled by automation and by approaches that seek to eliminate the need for follow-up. In an ideal world suppliers would perform exactly as required by the time required and no follow-up would be necessary. Until that happy day dawns, though, we must recognise that expediting is an essential part of purchasing work.

2.6 The importance of purchasing research has never been greater. The pace of change in the environment generally, and in supply markets in particular, make it essential to dedicate staff to monitoring activities. The objective is to improve the quality of buying by collecting, classifying and analysing relevant data to help in decision making. This area embraces economic forecasting, demand projections, analysis of prices and availability of materials, and analysis of potential suppliers.

2.7 Management of the purchasing function includes development of policies, procedures and controls; management of resources; the building of relationships within the purchasing and supply chain; and dealing with specific problems in supplier and commodity management.

Typical roles and responsibilities

2.8 The word 'typical' in this heading is important: naturally, there will be much variation in the way that roles and responsibilities are divided among staff members. In particular, such division will be much more a feature of large purchasing departments than small ones.

2.9 The following roles might be considered 'typical'. We will look at each of them in turn.

- Head of Purchasing
- Senior Purchasing Manager

- Purchasing Manager
- Contracts Manager
- Supplier Manager
- Expediter
- Purchasing Analyst
- Purchasing Leadership Team

Head of Purchasing

2.10 The Head of Purchasing may have a title such as Procurement Director. In many organisations, this will be a position on the main board.

2.11 As the job title suggests, the Head of Purchasing takes overall responsibility for all the work of the purchasing function. In particular, he provides strategic leadership in areas such as policy formulation. The strategic aspect of this role is vital, particularly in a large organisation. The Head of Purchasing should be able to rise above the day-to-day operational pressures in order to give overall direction to the work of the purchasing function.

2.12 In practice, it is unlikely that the Head of Purchasing will be able to exercise control over every aspect of purchasing. This is because it would be impractical in most organisations to centralise purchasing to such an extent. Even in a strongly centralised environment, there is always likely to be a role for user departments in purchasing routine, low-value items.

2.13 As head of the entire function, the Head of Purchasing is also responsible for representing the function in its dealings with other departments. This calls for strong leadership and communication skills, especially in the need to convey to other departmental heads the benefits offered by the purchasing function.

Senior Purchasing Manager

2.14 The Senior Purchasing Manager (SPM) will be next in seniority to the Head of Purchasing. Typically, he will be leader of a team of Purchasing Managers. His team leadership role will involve coordination of all activities undertaken by his subordinates.

2.15 The SPM will work within the strategic framework laid down by the Head of Purchasing. Following this guidance, he will be responsible for broad decisions on market evaluation, sourcing, appraisal and selection of suppliers, negotiations with suppliers, and award of contracts.

2.16 Depending on the organisational structure, the SPM may be responsible for just a single category of purchase (eg IT expenditure, or expenditure on raw materials or commodities), or alternatively his brief may extend across all categories of external spend. A relatively common structure in large organisations would involve an SPM in charge of one large category of expenditure, with a number of Purchasing Managers reporting to him, each of whom takes responsibility for a subdivision of the SPM's spending.

Purchasing Manager

2.17 The Purchasing Manager has responsibilities similar in scope to those of the SPM, though of course at a lower level. He may be a single individual, or one of several reporting to the SPM. Like the SPM, his role may be confined to a single category of spend, or it may be more wide-ranging. This largely depends on the size of the purchasing function as a whole.

2.18 The Purchasing Manager will not generally become involved in the day-to-day running of established contracts. His role typically ends with the award of a contract, leaving others to deal with subsequent contract management.

Contracts Manager

2.19 A Contracts Manager will be needed in cases where a large and complex contract has been awarded. In such a case it becomes important to manage all the issues specified in the contract: monitoring that supplier performance is up to standard, ensuring that payments to suppliers are made in line with the agreement, checking and approving changes to the contract if any are necessary.

2.20 This is a closely defined role, and the Contracts Manager will not become involved in wider issues. For example, general relations with the supplier are the province of the Supplier Manager; the Contracts Manager is concerned solely with ensuring that both parties fulfil their contractual obligations.

Supplier Manager

2.21 Once a contract has been awarded (typically by the Purchasing Manager) it becomes important to manage relations with the successful supplier. The Supplier Manager will be concerned to evaluate the supplier along a number of different dimensions (the term 'balanced scorecard' is sometimes used to describe this approach). For example, the supplier will be interested in quality management systems, supplier involvement in new product development, supplier development, information sharing etc.

2.22 To distinguish the roles of Contract Manager and Supplier Manager it is important to realise that there may well be more than one contract with any particular supplier. The Contract Manager will be concerned with strict compliance to the terms of a particular contract; the Supplier Manager will be concerned with broader aspects of the relationship with the supplier.

Expediter

2.23 As the name suggests, the role of the expediter begins once an order has been placed. At that point, it is rarely sufficient to sit back and trust that the supplier will deliver on time. More realistically, it will be necessary to expedite: ie to chase the supplier so as to ensure timely delivery of the correct items ordered. Without this, we risk late or inaccurate delivery, with damaging knock-on effects on production.

Purchasing Analyst

2.24 Purchasing analysis (or purchasing research) is a vital role in a large purchasing function. The role of the Analyst is to investigate the supply market, to gather data, and to organise it into information that can be used by other members of the purchasing team. This is essentially a support role for the purchasing function as a whole, and as such is sometimes neglected in all but the largest purchasing departments. The focus of the Analyst's attention may be on suppliers or on the items and materials purchased by the organisation.

Purchasing Leadership Team

2.25 As the name suggests, this is a team comprising senior members of the purchasing function, particularly in large organisations. The team is naturally led by the Head of Purchasing and provides a means by which he can communicate with the senior members of staff reporting to him. The focus of meetings will be on the strategic direction envisioned by the Head of Purchasing.

What do purchasers do?

2.26 Another way of looking at the purchasing task is to consider what it is that purchasers actually do. This may vary widely according to different departmental organisations, different role descriptions and different organisation types, but in general, the task of purchasing at an operational level includes the following activities.

- Supply market monitoring, and identifying potential sources of supply
- Supplier evaluation and selection
- Processing purchase or stock replenishment requests
- Providing input to the preparation of specifications (definition of requirements) for new purchases
- Negotiating, buying and developing contracts (settling terms and conditions of trade between the buyer and the seller)
- Expediting or contract management (ensuring that suppliers deliver according to the purchase order or contract)
- Clerical and administrative tasks: record keeping, report generation and processing of documentation through all of the above activities.

2.27 The operational task of purchasing is sometimes expressed as a cycle of activity called the **purchasing cycle**, which in a simple form may look something like Figure 2.2.

Figure 2.2 *The purchasing cycle*

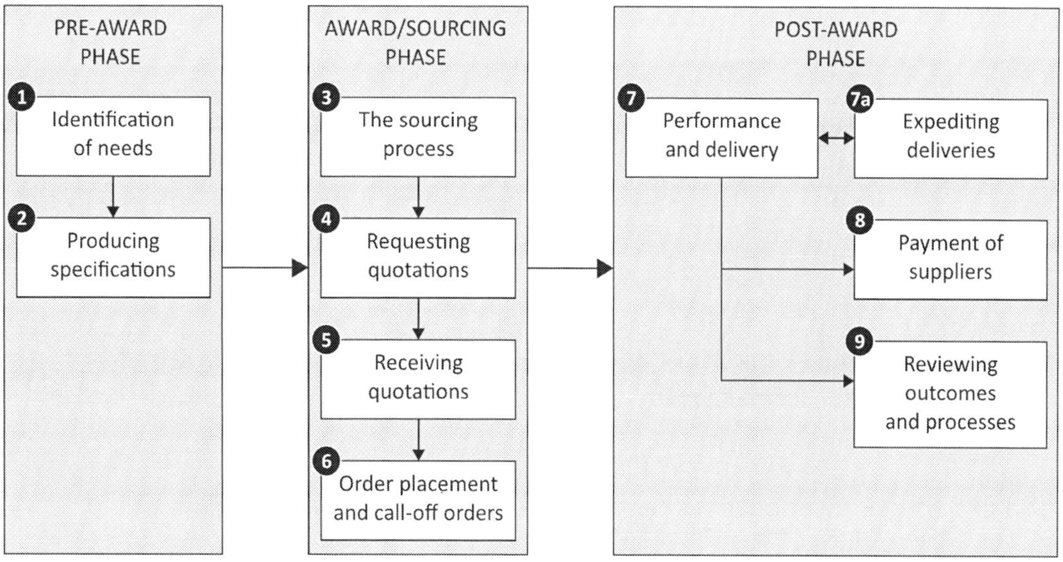

2.28 Chapter 7 of this Course Book covers the purchasing cycle and the tasks and procedures of purchasing in detail. In the meantime, don't be worried if some of the terms used in Figure 2.2 are not clear to you.

2.29 Finally, purchasing is an important interface between the organisation and the outside world. Purchasing staff must be careful to ensure that the image they promote is one that benefits the organisation. In particular, fair treatment of suppliers and the highest standards of ethical and environmental behaviour are essential.

3 Achieving value for money

Cost reduction strategy

3.1 Cost reduction will be a key objective to support the financial goals of the firm (profitability, liquidity, return on capital invested and so on), even in the public sector (with goals such as value for money service provision and efficiency targets). It will be the cornerstone of business strategies based on cost leadership (the strategy of selling more products by tempting customers with low prices).

3.2 Cost strategies are about knowing what the costs really are and then looking at how to reduce them. In other words, we must apply effective cost analysis. Then we are in a position to look at eliminating waste, negotiating on price and so on.

3.3 At a strategic level, supply chain management may secure cost reductions through measures such as the following.

- Restructuring: delayering, downsizing or horizontalising purchasing structures, to minimise labour and overhead costs and maximise process efficiencies (less duplication of effort, fewer managerial and co-ordinatory mechanisms, and so on)
- Centralising purchasing (to take advantage of larger orders and bargaining power) or decentralising purchasing (to reduce transport and storage costs)
- Process engineering or re-engineering, to streamline and integrate processes, eliminating unnecessary activities and process inefficiencies
- Outsourcing or off-shoring non-core competencies: where value can be obtained at less cost, the organisation can dispose of assets, and internal resources can be more efficiently focused
- Developing supplier relationships for cost and price advantages (whether by using competitive leverage to secure low prices or by developing collaboration to reduce sourcing and transaction costs, encourage mutual cost reduction and so on)
- Applying ICT and automation technologies to streamline processes and to increase productivity and reduce labour costs.

Trade-offs

3.4 There is frequently a trade-off between cost objectives and quality, service and delivery objectives. This has led to the recognition that cost/price and 'value' are not the same thing. 'Value for money' is an important strategic objective, particularly in the public and non-profit sector. It has been defined as 'the optimum combination of whole life cost and the quality necessary to meet the customer's requirement'.

3.5 A number of purchasing techniques can be used to obtain value for money.

- The use of value analysis (and/or value engineering of new products and processes), in order to eliminate non-essential features. This means looking critically at all the elements that make up a product or service and investigating whether they are really necessary, whether they could be done more efficiently or cheaply etc
- Consolidation of demand (eg by aggregating orders)

- Centralised negotiation of contracts and prices
- Proactive sourcing: challenging preferred supplier complacency to ensure competitive value. (Supply contracts may contain provision for year-on-year price reductions, for example, as an incentive to efficiency improvements.)
- Buying complete subassemblies rather than components
- Encouraging standardisation to reduce costs of spares and maintenance
- Adopting whole life costing methodologies (rather than focusing on purchase price). We will look at whole life costing later in this Course Book.
- Eliminating or reducing inventory (and therefore reducing costs of storage, holding, deterioration and obsolescence)
- Using e-procurement for process efficiencies
- Global purchasing (to take advantage of low-cost country production)

Reducing inventory costs and administration

3.6 Not all value additions arise from within the buyer's organisation. Buyers have a close relationship with external suppliers and are well placed to take advantage of any contribution that can be extracted from them.

3.7 One area in which this is possible is the management of inventory. Modern thinking suggests that 'inventory is evil'. This is because if an organisation holds stock it reduces the amount of cash available. We have paid money to acquire or manufacture the stock, and we do not recover the money until the stock is sold. Stock is also said to be a cover or disguise for inefficient work practices; if there were no buffer stock to fall back on we would have to remedy such inefficiencies, but with stock in hand we can afford to overlook them.

3.8 Few organisations (probably no organisation) would pursue this thinking to the point of holding no stock at all. But it is clear that minimising stock is an aid to operational efficiency, provided that we do not disappoint our customers for lack of stock.

3.9 This is an area where suppliers can assist. By working closely with suppliers, buyers can minimise the levels of stock needed. One technique is **just in time purchasing**. Suppliers do not deliver stock until the moment that the buying organisation actually needs it. This implies very close liaison with suppliers, who must be continually updated on production schedules.

3.10 Another technique is **consignment stocking**. This means that suppliers provide a buyer with stock, on the buyer's premises, but without charging for it in advance. Instead, the buyer pays for the stock only as he uses it. This protects the buyer's cashflow, while at the same time he benefits from having stock on hand – at the supplier's expense.

3.11 The buyer may still incur administrative and storage costs under this arrangement, but it can work out much cheaper than being charged for the stock as soon as it is delivered. And in some cases, even the administrative and storage costs may be passed on to the supplier. Some firms have an arrangement where the supplier maintains a small store on the buyer's premises, staffed by the supplier. As and when the buyer requires goods from the consignment stock, the supplier staff member handles the administration and paperwork.

3.12 From the supplier's point of view, this kind of arrangement has the advantage that he gains most or all of the buyer's business for the items stocked. He is sure of making an immediate sale when the requirement for his goods arises.

Collaboration on cost reduction

3.13 A further area where suppliers can assist the buyer in achieving his objectives is a joint initiative to reduce costs. This can best be illustrated in the context of a manufacturing company, although the principles apply elsewhere too.

3.14 An increase in the proportion of external spending by manufacturers means that many such companies can be described as 'low value added' firms. In other words, the price paid by the eventual consumer is largely made up of costs charged by suppliers to the manufacturer: the manufacturer himself adds relatively little value.

3.15 The implication of this is clear. To achieve competitive prices, such companies must focus on their costs, which increasingly arise outside the boundaries of the firm. Purchasing's contribution in reducing costs right along the supply chain, while maintaining and improving quality, is vital.

3.16 This will require a measure of trust, reflected in **open book costing**: suppliers should be ready to talk frankly with customers about their cost structures. This has several advantages: it facilitates cost-based pricing; enables the buyer to get to know the supplier's operations and processes (for closer collaboration); enables joint identification of areas for cost reduction and added value; and reassures buyers that they are receiving value for money (non-exploitative profit margins).

3.17 An even more radical approach is **cost transparency**, where there is two-way sharing of cost information on activities in which buyer and supplier have a common interest. This is more suited to a strategic partnership relationship (and even then, with appropriate confidentiality protection).

Payment and warranty terms

3.18 A supply contract of course contains many terms in addition to the basic purchase price. One area where buyers can exploit this is in the terms relating to payment and warranties.

3.19 In relation to payment, a buyer must do all he can (in conjunction with his colleagues in Finance) to honour any contract term relating to the due date for paying the supplier. But that does not stop him from negotiating hard for extended payment terms. Buyers sometimes underestimate the importance of this: 'If we have to pay the price anyway, what does it matter if we get 90 days credit rather than 60?'

3.20 The answer is that it matters a good deal. If we can delay payment by 30 days, it means that the money is working hard in our own bank account, perhaps earning interest on deposit, or reducing the amount that we pay in overdraft interest. This is much preferable to having the money in the supplier's account earlier than it needs to be. But we repeat that this should only be done within the terms of the supply contract. If the buyer wilfully delays payment beyond the due date, it will have a damaging effect on supplier relations.

3.21 Warranty terms are another area, often overlooked, where added value can be leveraged. We run a risk of disruption to operations, or having to compensate a disappointed customer, in the event of product failure. If such failure can be traced to an input purchased from a supplier, it is entirely appropriate that the supplier should bear the cost. A warranty term is one that places an obligation on the supplier in such circumstances to compensate the buyer in whole or in part. Buyers should look out for opportunities to include warranty terms in supply contracts.

4 Sustainability in procurement and supply

How sustainable procurement supports sustainable development

4.1 The procurement function has a key role to play in any organisation's contribution to national (and international) sustainable development strategy and commitments.

4.2 The procurement function is responsible for sourcing the inputs to organisational processes. As such, it can contribute to sustainable consumption by the organisation: ensuring that inputs are environmentally-friendly and ethically sourced. Of course, this is also a key contribution to sustainable production, which includes the sustainability of its inputs and sourcing processes.

4.3 Sustainable procurement is an approach that takes economic, environmental and social sustainability into account when making purchasing decisions. It's about looking at what purchased items are made of, where they come from, how they are made and by whom, how they will be used – and whether they are in fact necessary – to ask:

- Does procurement, in all these aspects, meet the present needs of the organisation, its customers and its wider stakeholders, without compromising the ability to continue to do so in future – by degrading the environment, depleting resources, undermining trading relationships and so on?
- Does procurement, in all these aspects, protect or enhance the economic viability of the organisation (by adding value, controlling costs, securing supply continuity, meeting the needs of internal and external customers, building beneficial supply chain relationships and so on), without negative environmental or social impacts?

Defining sustainable procurement

4.4 The United Nations' procurement website emphasises the full spectrum of economic, environmental and social criteria in its definition and explanation of sustainable procurement.

'Procurement is called sustainable when it integrates requirements, specifications and criteria that are compatible and in favour of the protection of the environment, of social progress and in support of economic development, namely by seeking resource efficiency, improving the quality of products and services and ultimately optimising costs.

Through sustainable procurement, organisations use their own buying power to give a signal to the market in favour of sustainability and base their choice of goods and services on:

- Economic considerations: best value for money, price, quality, availability, functionality;
- Environmental aspects, ie green procurement: the impacts on the environment that the product and/or service has over its whole lifecycle, from cradle to grave; and
- Social aspects: effects of purchasing decisions on issues such as poverty eradication, international equity in the distribution of resources, labour conditions, human rights.'

4.5 Meanwhile, CIPS itself has adopted the definition of sustainable procurement used by the Sustainable Procurement Task Force (SPTF). In *Procuring the Future*, the report of the UK's Sustainable Procurement National Action Plan, sustainable procurement is defined as:

'A process whereby organisations meet their needs for goods, services, works and utilities in a way that achieves value for money on a whole-life basis in terms of generating benefits not only to the organisation, but also to society and the economy, whilst minimising damage to the environment.'

The procurement function's contribution to sustainability

4.6 Broadly, the procurement function is well placed to exercise influence on sustainability because of its position at a crucial interface between the organisation and its external environment. It may have input to, or responsibility for, activities such as the following.

- The development and implementation of sustainable procurement strategies and policies
- The design and development of sustainable products and services (especially in situations where early buyer involvement is used, or where procurement can act as the interface with suppliers to develop early supplier involvement)
- The definition of requirements (in specifications, tender documents, contracts, purchase orders and service level agreements) to include sustainable materials, components, supplies and services
- The sustainable and ethical sourcing of products and services, building sustainability considerations into sourcing strategy – and each stage of the sourcing cycle (including supplier selection)
- The management of supply and logistics processes to minimise waste, transport and other environmental impacts, and to support reverse logistics, recycling, re-use and other measures. (This may, for example, include the development of lean supply.)
- The monitoring, management and development of suppliers (and supply chains) throughout the life of contracts and supply relationships, to support sustainability performance and improvement
- Monitoring, measuring and reporting on the sustainability of procurement (and related production and logistics issues), to help raise awareness, make the business case for sustainability, and manage overall corporate sustainability performance.

The 'triple bottom line'

4.7 One of the earliest and most respected advocates of corporate sustainability is John Elkington. In 1994, Elkington coined the term 'triple bottom line'.

4.8 Based on the accounting concept of 'the bottom line' (profit), the term was designed to engage business leaders, raising awareness that corporate activity not only adds economic value, but can potentially also add environmental and social value – and, more importantly, create environmental and social costs (previously regarded as 'externalities', not accounted for in the performance measurement of organisations). Traditionally, these have been borne financially by governments and experientially by communities: in TBL thinking, businesses which cause costly social and environmental impacts should share (or at least recognise) these costs.

4.9 The triple bottom line (also called TBL, 3BL, and later 'People, Profit, Planet') recognises the need for businesses to measure their performance not just by how well they further the interests of their primary stakeholders (shareholders) through profitability (the 'economic bottom line'), but also by how well they further or protect the interests of their secondary stakeholders (including wider society), in relation to social and environmental sustainability. TBL accounting means expanding the traditional reporting framework of a company to take into account ecological and social performance, in addition to financial performance.

Profit (economic measures)

4.10 Profit is the original bottom line. However, in a sustainability framework 'profit' implies the ongoing impact the organisation has on its economic environment. This is not the conventional, internal business measurement of profit, but a quantified, comparable measure of the lasting value added to the host society.

4.11 Beyond this strict definition, however, economic sustainability can embrace a number of commercial considerations such as: ethical trading, corporate governance, value for money, adding value, sustainable pricing and supplier negotiation, resource efficiency, risk-managed capital purchasing, and responsible budgetary control.

People (social measures)

4.12 The social dimension of sustainability relates to fair and beneficial business practices towards labour, the community and the region(s) in or with which a company conducts its business. A TBL organisation seeks to benefit many constituencies, and not to exploit or endanger them.

4.13 This may include issues such as: the preservation of the living conditions and amenities of communities; ethical treatment of labour (health and safety, fair pay and conditions); monitoring of subcontractors for labour exploitation (and child labour or slave labour, in developing countries); support for small and local businesses; support for diversity and equal opportunity in employment; development of skills; support for the use of local labour and the long-term unemployed; equitable gain sharing with supply chain members; and 'giving back' to communities (eg through investment, charitable giving and sponsorship).

Planet (environmental measures)

4.14 This relates to the more established area of sustainable environmental policies and practices, which seek either to benefit the natural environment or to minimise harmful impacts upon it.

4.15 This may involve: reducing pollution, waste and energy/resource consumption; minimising or repairing environmental damage (eg deforestation); controlling the disposal of harmful wastes; using renewable or recyclable materials and designs; reducing greenhouse gas (GHG) emissions and 'carbon footprint'; educating supply chains and customers to support environmental practices; investing in 'green' projects such as renewable energy, land reclamation and reforestation; and so on.

4.16 Profit, People, Planet considerations can be applied specifically to procurement activities, to illustrate the dimensions of sustainable procurement. Table 2.1 summarises some of procurement's key potential contributions in each area.

Table 2.1 *Potential for procurement to add value to the TBL*

Profit: adding economic value	• Securing value for money • Effective investment appraisal and capital purchasing • Cost management and budgetary control • Added value (through sourcing efficiencies, supplier involvement, quality improvement) • Ethical trading to support the long-term financial viability of suppliers and supply markets (including sustainable pricing, ethical tendering and negotiation, payment on time)
Planet: adding environmental value	• Input to design and specification of green products/services • Sourcing of green materials and resources • Green sourcing, including selection, management and development of suppliers with environmental capability and commitment • Reducing the waste of resources throughout the sourcing cycle • Managing logistics (including reverse logistics) to minimise waste, pollution, GHG emissions and environmental impacts (and to support re-use, recycling and safe disposal)
People: adding social value	• Encouraging purchasing team and supplier diversity • Monitoring supplier practices to ensure observance of human rights and labour standards (eg re slavery, child labour, conditions of work, health and safety, equal opportunity) • Input to health and safety of products/services (design, specification, supplier quality management) • Fair and ethical trading (fair pricing, ethical use of power, ethical business practices) • Local and small-business sourcing

5 Staff with devolved responsibilities

Centralisation and decentralisation of purchasing

5.1 An important organisational issue is the extent to which purchasing responsibilities should be centralised, ie placed in the hands of a single department reporting to a single executive.

5.2 One particular context in which this arises concerns service firms (firms such as banks, solicitors etc – providing services to their customers rather than tangible products). In such firms it is common to find that purchasing is carried out by users rather than by purchasing specialists. (And this practice is by no means confined to service firms.)

5.3 This situation gives rise to no real differences of opinion in the purchasing literature: almost without exception, commentators suggest that responsibilities for purchasing should lie as far as possible with purchasing specialists. Although user departments have an important role in decision making, actual selection of suppliers and processing of orders falls to the purchasing function.

5.4 The position is far more complex when multi-site operations are in question. Clearly, an organisation that operates through a number of branches or divisions, perhaps separated by considerable distances, may consider a single purchasing function at head office (centralisation) or separate functions at each division (decentralisation). The choice is rarely clear cut.

5.5 To begin with it is worth pointing out that the choice is not necessarily between two extreme possibilities. There is a spectrum of organisational arrangements bounded at one end by full centralisation and at the other by full decentralisation. In between, there are arrangements in which some activities are centralised while other matters are decided at local level. Most organisations operate somewhere in the middle of the spectrum rather than at its extremes.

Advantages of centralisation

5.6 A major advantage claimed for centralisation of purchasing is the greater specialisation that is possible among purchasing staff. If 100 purchasing staff are scattered around 10 divisions each of them must have general responsibility for a wide range of his division's requirements. General responsibilities lead to general knowledge, and highly specialised knowledge may be absent.

5.7 By contrast if 100 purchasing staff are based at a single centralised location, there is opportunity to divide tasks among them on the basis of specialised skills. Each buyer can focus on a particular area and develop his knowledge to greater depth. This has great benefits when a wide range of complex materials are required by the organisation.

5.8 A further advantage is that the requirements of different divisions can be consolidated. This reduces the frequency of very small orders for a particular material and enables buyers to obtain better prices and service. The number of suppliers is likely to be smaller, and order administration and processing is more streamlined. This advantage is particularly evident if the divisions are relatively small, because in such a case there is a high likelihood that their individual requirements might be for uneconomic amounts.

5.9 Greater coordination of purchasing activities may result from a centralised structure. For example, uniform purchasing policies and procedures can be introduced and standardisation is facilitated. Staff training and development can be undertaken systematically.

5.10 Centralisation generally enables greater **standardisation** of procedures and specifications, avoiding 'maverick' buying and requirements.

- Standardisation of procedures should enable greater consistency of action, better performance monitoring and management (against consistent measures), better control and improved compliance.
- Standardisation of specifications should enhance quality and efficiency in a number of ways: facilitating the consolidation of orders; larger (but fewer) orders, for economies of scale and reduced transaction costs; a reduced supplier base (with fewer 'specialist' requirements); reduced inventory and handling costs (less variety and greater utilisation); improved quality management (ease of inspection etc); simpler and more accurate ordering; and simpler internal and supply chain communication.

5.11 Finally, the vital area of purchasing research is often neglected if individual divisions are expected to carry it out. This is partly because it is a specialised area, and specialised skills may not be available at divisional level. Partly also it is because the need for divisional purchasing staff to conduct a wide range of activities may mean that some areas receive too little attention; purchasing research is often neglected in this scenario.

5.12 If purchasing is centralised, it is usual to establish the function at head office and to appoint an overall manager or director reporting at board level. Apart from operational buying, the function will handle planning, purchasing research, specialised buying, and negotiation of long-term contracts.

5.13 Centralised purchasing suffers from the disadvantage that communication is difficult. However, this can to some extent be countered by developing detailed purchasing manuals, arranging regular visits to divisions by central purchasing personnel, and by training courses emphasising group policies. Electronic links are also extremely important in overcoming this difficulty.

Advantages of decentralisation

5.14 Although the above ideas are powerful arguments for centralisation, things are rarely so clear cut as they might suggest. There are also significant advantages in **devolving** purchasing responsibilities to local level, which means allowing local units of the organisation to manage their own purchasing without relying on Head Office.

5.15 One reason for doing so is to maximise coordination between purchasing and operating departments. Buyers are close to users and develop a close understanding of their needs and problems. Face-to-face discussions are easy to organise and can help to crystallise problems and stimulate solutions.

5.16 Another benefit of decentralisation is that local buyers can respond more quickly to user needs. Centralised purchasing can run into difficulties if things do not go exactly according to plan. Reacting quickly to changes in schedules or unforeseen problems is easier if buyers are close to the scene of operations. Relying on long-distance communication inevitably means that response times are longer.

5.17 Locally based buyers also have the advantage of knowing locally based suppliers. There are great advantages – of cost, delivery time etc – in sourcing from short distances, and a centralised purchasing function will have difficulty in identifying good local suppliers.

5.18 Finally, there is an important management principle that supports a policy of decentralisation. This is the principle that a divisional manager can only be held accountable for the performance of his division if he has genuine control over its operations. This is not the case if the vitally important area of procurement is taken out of his hands and given instead to a centralised purchasing function.

5.19 If purchasing is carried out at local level, it is likely that there will still be a need for a centralised purchasing function to carry out specialised activities, such as purchasing research or buying of specialised materials. Often long-term contracts may be negotiated by the central purchasing office with divisional buyers calling off requirements against the contracts.

5.20 Lysons suggests that a mix of centralised and decentralised purchasing is common in practice. Both local and central purchasing functions exist, with a division of duties somewhat as indicated by Table 2.2.

Table 2.2 *Duties of local and central purchasing functions*

LOCAL PURCHASING FUNCTION	CENTRALISED PURCHASING FUNCTION
Small order items	Determination of major purchasing policies
Items used only by the local division	Preparation of standard specifications
Emergency purchases (to avoid disruption to production)	Negotiation of bulk contracts for a number of divisions
Items sourced from local suppliers	Stationery and office equipment
Local purchasing undertaken for social 'community' reasons, eg support for smaller, local suppliers	Purchasing research Staff training and development Purchase of capital assets

The part-time purchaser

5.21 As we have seen, there are advantages and disadvantages to centralising the purchasing function. We note that in practice there is a spectrum of possibilities between full centralisation and full decentralisation. Unless an organisation is at the extreme 'centralisation' end of the spectrum, part-time purchasing will be present. The term refers to purchasing activities undertaken by people who are not members of the purchasing function, and whose main activities are nothing to do with purchasing.

5.22 Why does part-time purchasing take place? There are three main reasons.

- In some organisations, part-time purchasing was a regular occurrence at a time before the introduction of a dedicated purchasing function. (Remember that the development of the purchasing profession is a relatively recent trend.) In such organisations, a legacy of part-time purchasing remains for historical reasons.
- Sometimes user departments believe themselves best qualified to make purchasing decisions. This is particularly the case where the items to be purchased are very technical in nature: users may not trust the purchasing function to have sufficient technical understanding.
- Finally, there is the phenomenon of 'maverick spending': users sometimes deliberately keep spending decisions away from the purchasing department. This may be because they simply wish to keep power in their own hands, or may reflect distrust of purchasing's objectives, which are sometimes perceived to be solely concerned with cost reduction.

Advantages and disadvantages of part-time purchasing

5.23 There are obvious disadvantages associated with part-time purchasing.

- There is a high risk of committing company funds unwisely if the people responsible for spending have no professional expertise.
- There is a risk that a part-time purchaser is too preoccupied with his main role to give sufficient attention to his purchasing activities.
- There are serious difficulties in budgeting and controlling spend if responsibilities for purchasing are dispersed throughout the organisation.

5.24 However, it would be foolish to disregard the existence of part-time purchasing, and given that it exists, it makes sense to identify any advantages that it may bring.

- In the case of routine, low-value purchases it may be sensible to devolve responsibility to user departments. This frees up time for professional purchasers to devote to more difficult tasks.
- It is no bad thing to take advantage of the technical skills and knowledge that may be spread throughout the organisation. Part-time purchasing, if properly controlled, is a way of achieving this.
- The purchasing function should be concerned to communicate purchasing disciplines as far as possible throughout the organisation. Once again, a properly controlled part-time purchasing operation may be a means to this end.

Chapter summary

- In modern organisations, at least in the manufacturing sector, a very large proportion of revenue earned is spent on buying in materials and services from outside. This means that the scope of purchasing activity is very wide.
- Purchasing has developed from being primarily a reactive and administrative function. Nowadays, purchasing staff typically take on important strategic responsibilities.
- Some of the typical job roles to be found in a purchasing function are Head of Purchasing, Senior Purchasing Manager, Purchasing Manager, Contracts Manager, Supplier Manager, Expediter, Purchasing Analyst and Purchasing Leadership Team.
- Purchasing staff are naturally concerned with achieving cost reductions, but it is important to bear in mind possible trade-offs between cost on the one hand and quality, service and delivery on the other.
- Procurement staff have an important role to play in sustainability.
- An important strategic decision is whether purchasing should be centralised or decentralised. Even in a highly centralised environment there will still be some area where local staff or part-time purchasers play a role.

Self-test questions

Numbers in brackets refer to the paragraphs where you can check your answers.

1 Explain how changes in a modern organisation's cost base have led to an increased profile for purchasing activities. (1.1–1.6)

2 Illustrate numerically how cost savings may lead to higher profit increases than increased sales revenue. (1.11)

3 List some of the core tasks of a purchasing function. (2.3–2.7)

4 Describe the role of (a) a Senior Purchasing Manager and (b) a Supplier Manager. (2.14, 2.21)

5 Suggest strategic measures by which supply chain management may achieve cost reductions. (3.3)

6 Describe (a) just in time purchasing and (b) consignment stocking. (3.9, 3.10)

7 Distinguish between open book costing and cost transparency. (3.16, 3.17)

8 What is meant by the 'triple bottom line'? (4.8)

9 What are the benefits of standardising purchasing procedures and specifications? (5.10)

10 Suggest advantages of decentralising purchasing. (5.14ff)

11 Give reasons why 'part-time purchasing' takes place. (5.22)

CHAPTER 3

Benefits of Effective Procurement

Assessment criteria and indicative content

1.3 Describe the benefits of effective procurement for organisations

- How effective procurement impacts on profitability – the profit contribution effect
- Creating savings and improving efficiency
- Budgets and budget monitoring
- How effective procurement helps achieve targets

Section headings

1 Procurement and profitability
2 Creating savings and improving efficiency
3 Budgets and budget monitoring
4 Procurement and targets

1 Procurement and profitability

Introduction

1.1 As we saw in the previous chapter, purchasing staff are responsible for a very large proportion of the money spent in an organisation. Any money that purchasing can save will make a direct contribution to the profitability and competitiveness of the organisation. An economical and effective purchasing system is an essential part of a successful organisation.

1.2 Conversely, any money wasted in purchasing will damage the profitability and the competitiveness of the organisation or reduce the ability of a public sector organisation to deliver effective services. Regarding waste, there are two important elements to consider.

- *Specification*. It is essential to buy the right product. Just one wrong digit in a part number can make the difference so buyers must always take care, even with routine orders. Sometimes there may be a breakdown in communications which leads to the wrong goods being ordered so it is important to make sure any communication is clear and precise. There is also the problem of over or under specifying the product. If a product is over-specified, cheaper options might be overlooked and buyers may end up paying for features they don't need. However, if it is under-specified the product may not meet the requirements.
- *Quantity*. Buying too much of a product may be tempting if it leads to bigger discounts. However, this is only useful if the company is able to use or sell the extra goods. Otherwise, it is a waste of money because it generates surplus stock (stock that the organisation is unable to use). Depending on the circumstances, surplus stock can be disposed of by reducing prices, by using the goods internally or by selling them for scrap. In the worst case, the company might need to pay someone to take them away. In some circumstances this might be beyond a buyer's control: products might only be sold in bulk or demand might drop unexpectedly.

However, buying more products than the company needs is a waste of money and should be avoided wherever possible.

1.3 The cost of purchasing itself can be very expensive and in some cases can exceed the cost of the products or services being bought. The cost of purchasing includes the cost of salaries for purchasing staff, the cost of computer hardware and software, the cost of office space to house purchasing staff, the administrative costs of placing orders and so on. Keeping the cost of purchasing to a minimum is one of the major challenges faced by both public and private sectors.

1.4 Purchasing can also affect an organisation's ability to satisfy its end customers' needs. There are three important elements here.

- *Quality*. If the purchasing department buys goods of an inferior quality in order to save money, the customer may be satisfied in the short term but not in the long term. No customer wants to return products for repair, even if they are under guarantee. If the product fails to live up to the customers' expectations, the result could be lost customers and a lost reputation. The quality of a product can be summed up as 'fitness for purpose' and 'conformity to specification'.
- *Quantity*. Although it is important not to buy too much of a product, there will be customer service issues if a company doesn't have enough in stock. There are few things more likely to annoy a customer – internal or external – than being unable to buy or use the goods they want.
- *Lead time*. The lead time of a product is the time it takes from the moment the need is identified to the time when the goods or services are ready to be used. It is composed of both internal lead time (the time it takes to make an order) and external lead time (the time it takes the supplier to deliver the goods from the moment he receives the order). In routine purchases, the external lead time is likely to be longer than the internal lead time but on one-off purchases, the internal lead time may be longer than the external. It is a function of purchasing to reduce both elements as far as possible.

1.5 Purchasing can affect an organisation's reputation as someone reliable to do business with as well as the amount of money it earns. Although profitability is important, loss of reputation is a catastrophe from which some organisations never recover. Sadly, even the public sector is not immune to problems in this area. There have been many difficulties surrounding the implementation of computerised systems which have caused a real loss of confidence in the ability of some public sector organisations to offer anything like the service which their customers expect.

How purchasing can affect profitability: the profit contribution effect

1.6 Profit is the difference between the selling price of a product (or the total revenue earned from selling a product) and the cost of producing the product. In other words, it is the gain or surplus left over after the manufacturer (or service provider) has paid all its costs. Profitability is the primary objective of most businesses in the private sector. And even in the public sector, where providing a good level of services is the highest priority, buyers must still ensure that costs are held within the level of funding available to the public sector organisation.

1.7 Both buyers and suppliers seek to make a profit – and this is what makes price an adversarial issue. If a buyer negotiates a price downwards, he is improving his profit potential (by lowering his costs) – but lessening the profit potential of the supplier (by lowering his revenue). If a seller negotiates a higher price, he is improving his profit potential (by raising his revenue) – but lessening the profit potential of the buyer (by raising his costs).

1.8 Both buyers and suppliers seek to make a profit for a number of reasons.

- Profit means that the business has covered its costs, and is not 'bleeding' money in losses. This is important for the business to survive in the long term.
- Profit belongs to the owners (or shareholders) of the business, as a return on their investment: a share of profits is paid to them in the form of a 'dividend' on their shares. Strong and consistent profits are therefore important to encourage shareholders to continue to invest in the company, and to maintain the share capital of the company through a high share price (reflecting market demand for the shares).
- Profits which are not paid to shareholders ('retained profits') are available for reinvestment in the development of the business, enabling the business to acquire assets, meet long-term borrowings, update plant and equipment and build up reserves for future contingencies – without the cost and risk of borrowing funds for these purposes.

1.9 While a buyer will want to maximise its profits for all these reasons, it is also important to allow suppliers to make a reasonable profit:

- In order to protect the security of supply: not creating financial instability for suppliers, or driving them out of business by squeezing their profit margins
- In order to protect the quality of supply: allowing suppliers the revenue and profits they require to maintain quality and develop their business (potentially, to the benefit of their customers)
- In the interests of corporate social responsibility (CSR) and sustainability: allowing suppliers reasonable profits in order to protect employment and supplier diversity, develop sustainable supply chains and so on.

Mark-ups and margins

1.10 Costs, profit and selling price are related in the following fairly obvious way (using illustrative figures for clarity).

	$
Total costs incurred by the supplier	80.00
Plus profit earned by the supplier	20.00
Equals selling price charged by the supplier	100.00

1.11 It is often convenient to indicate the profitability of a particular business, or a particular product, by expressing the profit as a percentage. We may choose to express the profit as a percentage of total costs, or as a percentage of selling price.

- When we express the profit element as a percentage of cost, we refer to it as a *mark-up*. In our example above, the mark-up is 25% on cost (because $20 is 25% of $80).
- When we express the profit element as a percentage of selling price, we refer to it as a *margin*. In our example, the margin is 20% on selling price (because $20 is 20% of $100).

The link between cost and price

1.12 The price at which a supplier provides a product can be called the selling price (if viewed from the supplier's perspective) or the purchase cost (if viewed from the buyer's perspective). Of course the supplier himself must buy supplies to use in the production of his product or service and also to run his business generally (eg administration costs).

1.13 Clearly there must be a relationship between a supplier's costs (what he pays to purchase supplies for his own operations) and his selling prices (what he charges his customers for supplying his own products to them). This is because the supplier must aim to make a profit by ensuring that the revenue he earns from selling products is greater than the costs he incurs in providing the products.

1.14 In some cases, suppliers take explicit note of this relationship when determining their selling prices. They do this by calculating their costs and adding an additional amount for profit. This technique is known as **cost-plus pricing**. It is not an exact science because there are various different ways in which costs may be calculated and also different ways in which the supplier may calculate the appropriate amount to add on for profit. But these refinements are beyond the scope of this unit.

1.15 While cost-based pricing approaches have the advantage of simplicity, they are limited in various ways.

- They ignore demand, competition and other influences on pricing. If demand for a product is high, the supplier can charge a higher price, regardless of what his cost levels may be. If competition is intense, the supplier may have to settle for a lower price (again, regardless of what his costs may be) in order to be competitive.
- Cost-based prices are quite inflexible, and do not take into account changes or trends in the external environment.
- The supplier may be ignoring potential profits. For example, for a premium branded product, the customer might be willing to pay much more than the price derived from cost-plus methods. Or if a supplier is successful in reducing its production costs, the savings will (theoretically) be passed on to customers, rather than leading to higher profits.

1.16 These are some of the reasons why suppliers more often use competitive and market-based pricing strategies. In other words, they try to assess the highest price that the market will bear. Even if this is very much in excess of the costs incurred by the supplier, he may be justified in charging such a price if the customers are prepared to pay. At the other extreme, if the market will bear only a low price, the supplier must be careful that the prices he charges at least cover his costs; otherwise, he will trade at a loss and eventually be forced out of business.

2 Creating savings and improving efficiency

In the organisation as a whole

2.1 The ways in which the purchasing function adds value to an organisation are many and various but will clearly depend to some degree on the organisational structure, business focus etc. The following areas are common ways in which purchasing can contribute to organisational effectiveness and increased profitability.

- Cost reduction initiatives – these can be viewed in the context of purchase spend efficiency (eg negotiating low prices from suppliers) and purchasing operational efficiency (via improved methods of working, or use of technology such as e-commerce to reduce costs arising from the purchasing process).
- Improving supplier performance – developing more effective supplier relationships. Successful outcomes in this area can subsequently lead to further waste removal initiatives along the supply chain.
- Effective new product introduction (NPI) – contributing to the efficiency of NPI via early

purchasing involvement (EPI) and early supplier involvement (ESI) initiatives. These activities can contribute towards both reduced costs and improved time-to-market for NPI projects.
- Quality improvement initiatives – involvement in continuous improvement initiatives, eg multi-functional teams to support supplier quality improvement projects.
- Knowledge management – keeping the organisation informed about key market developments (legislation and regulations, technology improvement, alternative supply markets, alternative services and materials etc)
- Waste management – consideration of 'cradle-to-grave' environmental needs and costs; informing the business of the implications related to changing rules and regulations.
- Risk management – contributing to the avoidance of organisational risk exposure via market intelligence, appropriate supplier pre-contract appraisal, formulation of contingency plans etc.

2.2 Purchasing can add value either by cutting costs (but without loss of quality or product features), or by operational efficiency (leading to superior quality or product features at no additional cost). Ideally, we aim to achieve both of these objectives: improved output at reduced cost.

2.3 Here are some of the ways in which purchasing can help.

- By selecting appropriate suppliers they can improve the quality of inputs, with consequent improvement in the quality of outputs.
- By effective negotiation and/or tendering they can reduce the cost of inputs.
- By effective management of purchasing operations they can reduce the cost of processing purchase transactions.
- By effective dialogue with user departments they can improve specifications so that purchasing needs are fulfilled more efficiently and at lower cost.
- By effective liaison with user departments and suppliers they can ensure that inputs surplus to requirements are eliminated.
- By effective inventory management they can minimise the costs of acquiring and holding stock.

2.4 In a newly developed purchasing function the initial emphasis may be on cost reduction, relating both to the cost of inputs and to the cost of running the purchasing function. (The focus is on improving **efficiency**.) In a more developed purchasing function, measures may be introduced for more strategic aspects of the role, such as supplier relationship management. (The focus is on improving **effectiveness**.)

2.5 Table 3.1 highlights some possible measures relating to both efficiency and effectiveness.

Table 3.1 *Efficiency and effectiveness of purchasing*

MEASURES OF PURCHASING EFFICIENCY	MEASURES OF PURCHASING EFFECTIVENESS
Basic purchase price of inputs	Quality of output
Cost of placing an order	Quality of service to customers
Cost of staffing the purchasing function	Achieving objectives within budget
Speed of transaction processing	Quality of supplier relationships
Use of information technology	Impact on profitability
Efficiency of organisational structure	Prompt delivery to customers
Efficiency of supplier management	

2.6 The above discussion is not exhaustive but is indicative of the range of mechanisms, both direct and indirect, by which purchasing can significantly add value to the organisation.

In the purchasing function specifically

2.7 In this section we are concerned with purchasing cost reduction programmes, in contrast to company-wide cost reduction programmes.

2.8 The purchasing function is increasingly seen as being strategic in nature. This contrasts with an earlier view, according to which purchasing was a clerical, reactive function, whose main task was to place orders with suppliers. The new strategic perspective implies that purchasing must add value and contribute to business profitability. They do this by containing costs, or – better still – reducing costs.

2.9 A traditional approach to cost reduction by purchasing has involved squeezing suppliers. Typically, the supplier is offered the business if he agrees to reduce prices by an agreed amount. Whilst this approach may initially appear to be successful, in the longer term it often results in lower levels of supplier service, decreased quality, decreased supplier morale and increased administrative costs.

2.10 Another traditional purchasing ploy to reduce costs involves sourcing from an alternative low-cost provider. Again, this can show superficial cost reduction achievements but the reality in the longer term is something different. Often, total costs to the business increase through less obvious disruptive costs that quickly compromise efficiency.

2.11 Historically, many purchasing cost reduction initiatives have been conducted in a functional and isolated manner. Departmental targets have often been achieved at the expense of overall corporate objectives on profitability. By contrast, if cost reduction initiatives are developed in an integrated manner they have significant potential to reduce total cost throughout the supply chain, without any negative consequences to the business.

2.12 The traditional technique whereby purchasing impose demands for lower prices is to be avoided. The supplier often has no real means to lower costs and therefore behaves in a predictable manner: he cuts his own profit margins, or attempts to pass on the cuts to his own suppliers, or sacrifices quality.

2.13 The net result is a demoralised supply chain where suppliers are faced with diminishing returns. Predictably, such suppliers will not be very receptive or cooperative to participate in ongoing supply improvements and cost reduction exercises.

Five steps to purchasing cost reduction

2.14 This suggests that purchasing should adopt a more structured, integrated approach to cost reduction. The actual detail of such initiatives will clearly vary from company to company. However, the following five-step approach attempts to provide a general framework from which individual initiatives can be developed.

Step 1: understand the drivers for reducing cost

2.15 Purchasing and other stakeholders must be fully committed to the cost reduction process. They therefore need to fully understand where the drivers for reduced cost are coming from. To ensure clear understanding at the outset, purchasing should engage in a meaningful communications exercise.

Step 2: understand why excess costs exist in the supply chain

2.16 At the outset of cost reduction exercises it is useful to have some understanding of why 'excess' supply costs exist in the first place. This can be useful intelligence for subsequent stages of the project. Here are some possible reasons for excess costs in the supply chain.

- Passing on increased costs – this has been described as the 'french fries principle'. The consequences of a bad potato harvest are immediately passed on to the next in line of the supply chain who passes this on to the end customer of French fries. Conversely, the consequences of a good potato harvest mean a reduction in the supply price of potatoes but this reduction is rarely passed on to the end consumer of French fries.
- Over-specification – this is particularly relevant where products and services have been designed by isolated functions such as R & D. This often results in excess costs being incurred through over-specification.
- Supply cartels – despite various legislative directives, there is still much evidence of inflated supply prices as a consequence of supply market cartels (suppliers colluding with each other to stifle competition and maintain artificially high prices).
- Mechanistic bidding – traditional 'poker style' negotiation processes where suppliers artificially increase prices in advance of some concessionary negotiation tactics.
- Traditional buyer-supplier relationships – adversarial relationships have meant that the potential to reduce supply costs has remained largely untapped.

3

Step 3: supplier segmentation

2.17 Buyers should consider supplier segmentation models to ensure appropriate cost focus. In other words, they should distinguish between suppliers in choosing the kind of relationship they wish to establish with each one. For suppliers of critical items, a close collaborative relationship may be appropriate. For suppliers of routine items, a more traditional adversarial relationship, based on tough negotiation for the lowest possible price, may be more appropriate.

Step 4: cost reduction strategy and tactics

2.18 This involves developing the appropriate strategies and tactics to achieve ongoing total cost reductions along the supply chain.

Step 5: performance measurement and review

2.19 Cost reduction programmes should be viewed as dynamic processes. The alignment of purchasing initiatives with overall business strategy is essential. However, as business priorities change then so must the alignment and focus of cost reduction programmes.

2.20 Finally, it is important to measure the effectiveness of the cost reduction initiative. Appropriate measures should be established to demonstrate the effectiveness of the actions taken. This should be reviewed to highlight where successes have been achieved, with good practices being cascaded throughout the supply chain.

3 Budgets and budget monitoring

Definitions

3.1 A budget is a plan expressed in monetary terms. It is prepared and approved prior to the budget period (the period of time over which it describes how the organisation's money is going to be used) and may show income, expenditure and the capital to be employed.

3.2 Budgetary control is the establishment of budgets relating the responsibilities of executives to the requirements of a policy, and the continuous comparison of actual with budgeted results, either to secure the objectives of that policy or to provide a basis for its revision.

3.3 In general, budgets are set for specific periods of time in the future, for example the budget for the coming year. Sometimes budgets are constructed for specific projects that are to be undertaken, but again these can be analysed into the periods of time that the projects are expected to last. Thus, if a project is planned to last two years, the total budget for it can be split into that relating to the first year and that relating to the second year.

3.4 Budgets are plans expressed in financial and/or quantitative terms either for the whole of a business or for the various parts of a business for a specified period of time in the future. The budgets are prepared within the framework of objectives and policies that have been determined by senior management as part of its own planning activities.

Functions of budgetary control

3.5 Essentially the budgetary control (or **budget monitoring**) process consists of two distinct elements.

- **Planning**. This involves setting the various budgets for the appropriate future period. Managers at the various levels in an organisation should be involved in the budgetary planning stage for their own areas of responsibility. In many medium and large businesses this activity can take a considerable amount of time. There is a need to coordinate the budgets of the various parts of a business to ensure that they are all complementary and in line with overall company objectives and policies.
- **Control**. Once the budgets have been set and agreed for the future period under review, the formal control element of budgetary control is ready to start.

3.6 This control involves comparison of the plan in the form of the budget with the actual results achieved for the appropriate period. Significant divergences between the budgeted and the actual results should be reported to the appropriate managers so that the necessary action can be taken.

3.7 It is clear that the budget process will involve the prediction of future costs. To do this effectively it is important to understand the nature of the costs in question, and in particular whether the cost is fixed or variable. (Analysis of costs incurred in the past will help with this.)

- A **fixed cost** is one that does not vary in line with the level of activity. For example, the amount we pay in factory rental does not go up or down depending on how many widgets we produce. It is a fixed amount for the year, regardless of how busy we are.
- A **variable cost** is one that increases or decreases in line with the level of activity. For example, the cost of raw materials used in a manufacturing process is variable. If we are very

busy, we will need to buy lots of raw materials; whereas if business is slack our requirement for raw materials is less and the cost of purchasing them will be lower.

Fixed and flexible budgets

3.8 A **fixed budget** is based on a particular estimate of activity levels. For example, it may assume that sales volume will be 200,000 units in the coming year. The revenue and costs shown in the budget will all be based on this assumption. The problem arises when the assumption turns out to be wrong.

3.9 Suppose that an unexpected opportunity arises to increase production by 50,000 units because of a sudden surge in sales demand. This is obviously good news for the business, but it means that the fixed budget is no longer much use as a control tool.

3.10 For example, it is likely that we are going to be overspending all of our estimates of costs. While this would normally cause concern, in this case it is just an inevitable consequence of the increased production. The budget is sending the signal that we are overspending, whereas the truth is that we are doing well.

3.11 To cope with this problem businesses use **flexible budgets** in preference to fixed budgets. A flexible budget is a budget which, by recognising different cost behaviour patterns, is designed to change as volume of output changes. In the example above, as soon as we know that sales are way ahead of target all of the variable costs of sales are automatically revised on the flexible budget. Fixed costs of course are not altered. That is one reason why it is important to be able to distinguish fixed from variable costs.

The budgeting cycle

3.12 Any organisation will have a budget cycle: an ongoing and repeating process by which budgetary data is collected and analysed, budgetary targets are agreed (in line with overall objectives of the organisation) and budgetary statements are prepared and agreed.

3.13 The **budget period** is typically the same as the organisation's financial year. For control purposes, the annual budget will be broken down into smaller units, say months, but it is usual to begin by looking at annual figures.

3.14 It is normal to budget on an **incremental** basis. This means that the previous period's figures are taken as a starting point, and adjusted to take account of any known changes in circumstances (for example, if a supplier has announced a forthcoming increase in the cost of a material).

3.15 This takes place some time before the beginning of the budget period. Departmental managers then submit their budgets to the finance department, usually with a description of the key assumptions they have made and a justification of their figures.

3.16 It is the responsibility of the finance department to look at all departmental budgets and to review them in the light of overall organisational objectives. Often this will lead to a certain amount of iteration, with finance referring back to individual departments for possible amendments.

3.17 Eventually the overall organisational budget is settled, and the consequential departmental budgets are passed back to the managers concerned. The managers are thus aware of the limits on their authority to commit the organisation to expenditure.

3.18 Once the budget period is underway, there will be a process of regular review. Actual outcomes will be compared with budgeted figures and any significant variances will be investigated for control purposes. At defined periods (say quarterly) it may be necessary to take this one step further and produce a revised estimate of likely outcomes for the entire period. As the next budget period approaches, the cycle begins again.

Calculation of budget variances

3.19 The differences between the budgeted amounts and actual amounts are known as **variances**. Where they relate to costs (rather than revenue), if the actual cost is less than the budget cost the variance is described as favourable; if the actual cost is greater the variance is said to be adverse.

Example

3.20 Bug Ltd manufactures one uniform product only. The following statement shows the departmental overhead budget based on an average level of activity of 20,000 units of production per four week period, and the actual results for four weeks in October.

	Budget average for four week period	*Actual for 1 to 28 October*
	$	*$*
Indirect labour	20,000	19,540
Consumables	800	1,000
Depreciation	10,000	10,000
Other overheads	5,000	5,000
	35,800	35,540

3.21 You are required to produce an analysis of the variances between budget and actual.

Solution to the example

	Average four-week budget	*Actual results*	*Variances favourable/(adverse)*
	$	*$*	*$*
Indirect labour	20,000	19,540	460
Consumables	800	1,000	(200)
Depreciation	10,000	10,000	—
Other overheads	5,000	5,000	—
	35,800	35,540	260

3.22 In this case, we see that we have underspent our budget for indirect labour by $460, whereas with consumables we are $200 over our budget.

Types of budget

3.23 There are various ways of establishing budget targets.

- With an **incremental budget** we begin by looking at the actual figures for the previous period. We then adjust in line with known changes to arrive at a budget for the current period.
- With a **zero-based budget** we ignore previous periods and start completely from scratch.
- With a **priority based budget** we allocate funds in line with strategic goals.

3.24 Whichever of these methods is used, it is important to keep the budget up to date. Two techniques are worth mentioning in this context.

- A **rolling budget** is usually maintained. For example, a 12-month budget may be constructed for the period January to December. At the end of January, we update this by adding figures for the following January. Our revised budget then still covers a 12-month period, from February to January inclusive.
- At intervals during the year it is common to revisit the budget and update it in line with new information. This is sometimes referred to as producing a **forecast**.

Using computers in budgeting

3.25 The nature of the budgeting exercise is that many of the resulting final values are dependent on the estimate made of sales volumes, together with a few policy decisions (for example stockholding policies, payment period policies).

3.26 It is also true to say that budgets are a planning device designed to assist in the achievement of an organisation's longer-term plans.

3.27 These two factors have the following consequences.

- There are likely to be a number of alterations made to the first draft of the budget to see the effects of such changes.
- The alteration of one value will cause many other values to alter.

3.28 It is these factors which have led to the preparation of budgets being computerised, using spreadsheet packages. A spreadsheet is a computer package which stores data in a matrix format where the intersection of each row and column is referred to as a cell. Columns are referenced alphabetically and rows numerically with the result that a cell reference is a combination of these.

3.29 Each cell within a spreadsheet may be used to store:

- a label (description), eg the title of the spreadsheet
- a value, or
- a formula.

3.30 The formula is used to carry out calculations on values entered in other parts of the spreadsheet. The benefit of using formulae is that if some value on the spreadsheet is changed – eg the forecast of sales volume may be amended – the computer automatically recalculates all the formulae. In an instant the effect of the new assumption is displayed in the budget without any manual recalculation.

4 Procurement and targets

Goals, objectives and targets

4.1 Most writers agree with the idea that there is a hierarchy of objectives in organisations, just as there is a hierarchy of managers. The objectives at the top of the hierarchy are relevant to all aspects and members of the organisation, at a general level: they cascade down to the more specific objectives of business units, groups and individuals. The terms commonly given to the statement of objectives at each stage of this cascade can be pictured as follows: Figure 3.1.

Figure 3.1 *Hierarchy of objectives*

4.2 The **mission** of an organisation is a broad definition of the purpose of the organisation: what business are we in? what are we trying to achieve? The organisation's mission statement is usually a brief statement of the purpose, business areas and key cultural values of the organisation, stated in qualitative rather than quantitative terms. Its purpose is primarily to communicate a sense of meaning and direction to the people inside the organisation, as a guideline for activity.

4.3 Goals and objectives transform the mission or vision into targets or aims which the organisation will pursue. The terms are often used interchangeably, but it may be helpful to think of goals as statements of a desired future state ('where we want to get to'), and objectives as more specific, time-assigned, quantified targets to pursue in order to achieve each goal ('what we need to do to get there'). Effective objectives are often quantified using the mnemonic SMART: specific, measurable, attainable, relevant and time-bounded (ie with an agreed timetable for achievement).

4.4 To clarify, therefore:

- Mission: why the organisation exists
- Vision: the desired future state of the organisation
- Goals: the secondary and mainly narrative objectives derived from the mission and vision
- Corporate objectives: time-assigned, quantified aims derived from the goals

Aligning purchasing strategy with corporate strategy

4.5 Having established the corporate strategy it is logical to seek alignment between this and the strategies for functional departments, such as purchasing. To develop alignment it is necessary to translate corporate objectives into 'SMART' purchasing goals (Specific, Measurable, Attainable, Relevant, Time-bounded).

4.6 Specific examples of this translation process are shown in Table 3.2.

Table 3.2 *Translating corporate objectives into purchasing goals*

CORPORATE OBJECTIVES	PURCHASING GOALS (THIS FINANCIAL YEAR)
Become a low-cost producer within the market	Reduce like-for-like purchase spend by 20%
Introduce lean business practice	Reduce raw material stockturns to a maximum of 10 days
Focus on business core competencies	Outsource defined non-core-competency activities via new accredited suppliers
Improve time-to-market for new product development	Introduce early supplier involvement (ESI) initiatives for all key suppliers
Improve customer service levels via increasing quality of services and products	Introduce supplier development initiatives for identified material receipts of defects greater than 500 parts per million (ppm)

4.7 Procurement is effective when it furthers the organisation's goals, objectives and targets, as indicated in Table 3.2.

Conflicting targets

4.8 Sometimes the various objectives and targets of purchasing will come into conflict. For example, it is obvious that a low purchase price may be inconsistent with obtaining the highest quality materials. Similarly, the objective of speedy delivery from suppliers may be inconsistent with high quality or low price or both.

4.9 In such cases, it is the task of purchasing (working with user departments) to strike an appropriate balance between competing objectives. Usually, the key will be to identify which objective takes priority in the prevailing circumstances.

Chapter summary

- Purchasing staff have an important influence on organisational profitability. They control large sums of money spent with external suppliers, and the costs of the purchasing function themselves may also be very significant.
- Suppliers will sometimes relate their selling prices specifically to their input costs (cost-based pricing); however, it is more common to set prices on the basis of 'what the market will bear'.
- Purchasing can contribute to both the efficiency and the effectiveness of their organisations.
- Budgetary control is the process of planning and controlling costs and revenues. It is important to distinguish between fixed and variable costs, and to use this distinction in establishing flexible (rather than fixed) budgets.
- The goals established for a purchasing function must be aligned with overall organisational goals.

Self-test questions

Numbers in brackets refer to the paragraphs where you can check your answers.

1 How may the elements of specification and purchase quantities affect the issue of waste in the supply chain? (1.2)

2 Give reasons why both buyers and suppliers seek to make profits. (1.8)

3 Distinguish between a profit mark-up and a profit margin. (1.11)

4 List common areas where purchasing can contribute to organisational effectiveness and increased profitability. (2.1)

5 List ways in which purchasing can help to achieve improved output at reduced cost. (2.3)

6 List five steps in a structured approach to purchasing cost reduction. (2.14ff)

7 Define a budget. (3.1)

8 Distinguish between a fixed cost and a variable cost. (3.7)

9 What is meant by a budget variance? (3.19)

10 Give examples of how a purchasing goal can contribute to an overall organisational objective. (Table 3.2)

CHAPTER 4

The Five Rights of Procurement and Supply

Assessment criteria and indicative content

1.4 Identify the five rights of procurement and supply

- The five rights of procurement and supply
- Price/total cost, quality, timing, quantity and place
- Defining value for money

Section headings

1 Introduction to the five rights
2 Price/total cost of supplies
3 Quality of supplies
4 Timing of supplies
5 Quantity and place of supplies
6 Value for money

1 Introduction to the five rights

1.1 The primary task of purchasing is to provide the 'right' inputs for the organisation's processes. The 'right' inputs are traditionally described as follows.

- Inputs of the right quality
- Delivered in the right quantity
- To the right place
- At the right time
- For the right price

1.2 These are often called the five rights of purchasing.

1.3 The five rights are a traditional formula expressing the basic objectives of purchasing, and the general criteria by which purchasing performance is measured. Even if they are not called 'five rights', they are often covered in purchasing literature as 'key purchasing variables' (as in Baily et al) or 'purchasing factors' (as in Lysons & Farrington). Essentially, we are all talking about the same thing. We will give a brief overview of their nature and importance here.

1.4 The five rights (or five Rs) of purchasing, and the importance of achieving them, are summarised in Table 4.1.

Table 4.1 *The five rights of purchasing*

RIGHT	DESCRIPTION	IMPORTANCE
Quality	Obtaining goods which are of satisfactory quality and fit for their purpose (suited to internal and external customer's needs), by: • Accurate specification of requirement and quality standards • Supplier- and buyer-side quality management	If not achieved: • Stock may have to be rejected or scrapped • Production machinery may be damaged • Finished products may be defective and have to be scrapped or re-worked • Defective products may reach customers, resulting in recalls, returns, compensation claims, lost goodwill, damaged reputation • The firm will incur high costs
Quantity	Obtaining goods in sufficient quantity to meet demand and maintain service levels while minimising excess stock holding (which incurs costs and risks), by: • Demand forecasting • Inventory management • Stock replenishment systems	If not achieved: • Insufficient stock may be held to meet demand. Stockouts may cause bottlenecks or shutdowns in production; costs of idle time; late delivery to customers; lost credibility, goodwill and sales • Excess stock may be ordered and/or held: tying up capital in 'idle' stock; wasting storage space; risking deterioration, theft or damage; risking obsolescence or disuse; incurring 'holding costs'
Place	Having goods delivered to the appropriate delivery point, packaged and transported in such a way as to secure their safe arrival in good condition, by: • Distribution planning • Transport planning • Packaging	If not achieved: • Goods may be delivered to the wrong place, creating delay and correction costs • Goods may be subject to unnecessary transport and handling (and related costs) • Goods may be damaged, contaminated or stolen in transit • Transport may cause unnecessary environmental damage
Time	Securing delivery of goods at the right time to meet demand, but not so early as to incur unnecessary inventory costs, by: • Demand management • Supplier management	If not achieved: • Goods may be too late, causing production bottlenecks (and associated costs) and/or delays in delivery to customers (with costs of damages, lost business) • Goods may be too early, causing undue risks and costs of holding inventory
Price	Securing all of the above at a price which is reasonable, fair, competitive and affordable. Ideally, minimising procurement costs in order to maximise profit, by: • Price analysis • Supplier cost analysis • Competitive pricing and negotiation	If not achieved: • Suppliers will be free to charge what they like, without check • Supplier profit margins will be 'squeezed' unfairly, leading to insecurity of supply • Materials and supply costs will rise • Profits will fall – or prices charged to customers will have to rise (losing sales) • There will be less profit to motivate shareholders and reinvest in the business

1.5 It is worth noting that while achieving the five rights may be essential for effective purchasing, it may not be sufficient for the organisation's objectives and aspirations. There may be additional objectives to consider.

- **Relationship development**: developing collaborative long-term relationships with suppliers, not just for the immediate supply contract, but for ongoing partnership and mutual advantage

- **Innovation and development**: not just 'right quality' now, but potential to come up with innovative products and processes, and make collaborative quality improvements over time
- **Ethics and corporate social responsibility**: ethical trading, social sustainability (eg using small local suppliers) and environmental protection (eg purchasing of environmentally friendly supplies) – which may not always be compatible with 'right price', for example.
- **Total costs of ownership** of purchased items (especially large capital items such as machinery and equipment): not just 'right price' (purchase price), but the best total value package, including costs of installation, training, maintenance and repair, upgrading, insurance and so on.

1.6 It is especially worth noting that the five rights formula doesn't include 'the right supplier' – although selection of the right supplier will be crucial in achieving the other purchasing objectives. Arguably, the 'right supplier' is one who can deliver the right quantity and quality to the right place at the right time at the right price. However, there may be other considerations in the choice of supplier, such as the supplier's compatibility with the buying organisation; its credibility and reliability; its potential for innovation and development; its willingness to commit to continuous improvement and relationship development; its ethical and environmental performance; and so on.

Interrelationships and trade-offs between the five rights

1.7 It is also important to realise that the five rights are interdependent and interlinked, in all sorts of ways. Sometimes you can't get one without the other, and sometimes you can't get both at the same time. Here are some examples.

- If you don't get the right quality, you aren't getting the right quantity (because some items will be rejected or scrapped), at the right time (because delays will be caused by inspections and re-works), or the right price (because poor quality does not represent value for money, and incurs costs).
- On the other hand, high quality goods take a longer time to specify, produce and inspect (to manage the quality) – and if you don't get goods at the 'right time', high quality may be irrelevant: you may already have disrupted production and disappointed customers. Some corners may need to be cut on quality for 'urgent' requirements.
- The concepts of right quantity and right time are highly interdependent. You can have large quantities delivered early, in order to be sure to have sufficient items in stock – or you can have small 'top up' quantities delivered at the last minute, when you have a more accurate idea of demand (or even in response to demand, in a just in time system).
- There is often a trade-off between the right price and the other rights. Higher quality specifications cost more, as do short lead times (or 'urgent' orders) and complex delivery requirements (eg multiple deliveries). Quantity is a more complex trade-off. In terms of acquisition costs, frequent small orders may actually cost more (because of the extra transaction and transport costs) than fewer, large orders (subject to bulk discounts). However, fewer, larger orders will incur higher stock holding costs (such as storage and insurance). So the quantity/time factor will also have to juggle price considerations.
- Failure in any one aspect will impact on the others – and on purchasing's overall performance.

1.8 In the sections that follow we look in more detail at each of the five rights in turn.

2 Price/total cost of supplies

What is the 'right price'?

2.1 There is a temptation for buyers to think of the 'right' price simply as the lowest price – especially if the purchasing function's performance is judged on the basis of cost control or cost reductions. But, as we will see, this is not always the case. The aim of purchasers will be to secure the best or lowest price consistent with achieving all the other 'rights', and there is frequently a trade-off involved. You can probably get your goods faster, but at a higher price. You can probably get your goods cheaper, but at a lower quality. If you buy in higher quantities, you may get a bulk discount on the price – but will also incur higher costs of holding stock.

2.2 Price may be defined as 'the value of a commodity or service measured in terms of the standard monetary unit' (Lysons & Farrington). In other words, price is what a supplier charges for goods or services – and if two suppliers quote different prices, a purchaser can readily compare the relative value offered by each.

2.3 So what does it mean to buy at the 'right' price? The purchasing firm will be seeking to make a profit. It may also be seeking specifically to control or reduce its costs – and may expect the purchasing function to play a major part in this by reducing the cost of obtaining materials, goods and services. So the 'right' price may simply be the lowest price available.

2.4 However, remember that we have already established the need to buy goods of the right quality, in the right quantity, at the right time, delivered to the right place. The 'right' price will therefore be the best or lowest price available, consistent with ensuring the right quality, quantity, timing and delivery. In other words, what the purchaser is after is **value for money** – not just a 'cheap' price.

2.5 In fact, there are a number of other requirements for the 'right price', seen from the supplier's point of view as well as from the buyer's point of view.

Sales price

2.6 The 'right price' for the supplier or seller to charge (the right selling price) will be:

- A price which 'the market will bear': that is, a price that the market or a particular buyer will be willing to pay
- A price which allows the seller to win business, in competition with other suppliers (according to how badly it needs the business, and the prices being charged by its competitors)
- A price which allows the seller at least to cover its costs, and ideally to make a healthy profit which will allow it to survive in business and to invest in growth.

Purchase price

2.7 The 'right price' for the buyer to pay (the right purchase price) will be:

- A price which the purchaser can afford: allowing it to control its costs of production and make a profit on sale of its own goods or services
- A price which appears fair and reasonable, or represents value for money, for the total package of benefits being purchased
- A price which gives the purchaser a cost or quality advantage over its competitors, enabling it to compete more effectively in its own market

- A price which reflects sound purchasing practices: requiring suppliers to price competitively; negotiating skilfully; recognising the difference between strategic (or critical) and non-critical (or routine) purchases; and so on.

Understanding costs

2.8 It may seem like an obvious point, but it is important to distinguish clearly between 'price' and 'cost' – especially when reading exam questions! Price, as we have seen, is what a seller charges for a package of benefits offered to a buyer. Cost is what the buying organisation pays to acquire and utilise the goods purchased: as we have seen, this may be much more than just the purchase price paid to the seller. Moreover, the seller also has costs: the finance and resources it expends in producing and providing goods and services. And a buyer cannot routinely expect the (purchase) price of goods to be the same as their cost (of production) – otherwise, the supplier would not make a profit, and would be unlikely to survive.

Purchasing price and total cost of ownership

2.9 There is a delicate balance between 'the right price' and the other four 'rights' of purchasing, which professional buyers must be adept in managing. The overall objective can still be stated in terms of improving the profitability of the business, but 'profit' in this sense means any benefit, and particularly long-term benefits, accruing to the organisation – such as security and continuity of supply, innovation and quality improvements gained from developing partnerships with suppliers, and so on.

2.10 Even if we focus on costs, the modern view is that 'cost' is a far broader concept than simple purchase price. Current thinking emphasises a 'total cost of ownership' or 'total acquisition cost' which includes a package of costs not immediately apparent from the purchase price.

2.11 We said earlier that the 'right price' is one which represents value for money for the 'total package of benefits' being purchased. This is a very important point. There is a vital difference between the purchase price of an article and its *total acquisition cost* or *total cost of ownership*. Total acquisition cost includes not just the price of the items being purchased, but also:

- Various transaction costs, such as taxes, foreign exchange rate costs and the cost of drawing up contracts
- Finance costs (if capital has to be borrowed to pay for the purchase, say)
- The costs of packaging, transporting and insuring the goods for delivery
- Costs of storage and other handling, assembly or finishing required
- Costs of quality (inspection, re-work or rejection, lost sales, compensation of customers etc)
- Costs of installation, maintenance and repair (where relevant, eg for equipment purchases), staff training and so on, over the lifetime of the purchase.

2.12 Baily, Farmer, Jessop and Jones suggest that there is a 'price/cost iceberg', of which purchase price is only the most obvious or visible 'tip': Figure 4.1.

Figure 4.1 *The price-cost iceberg*

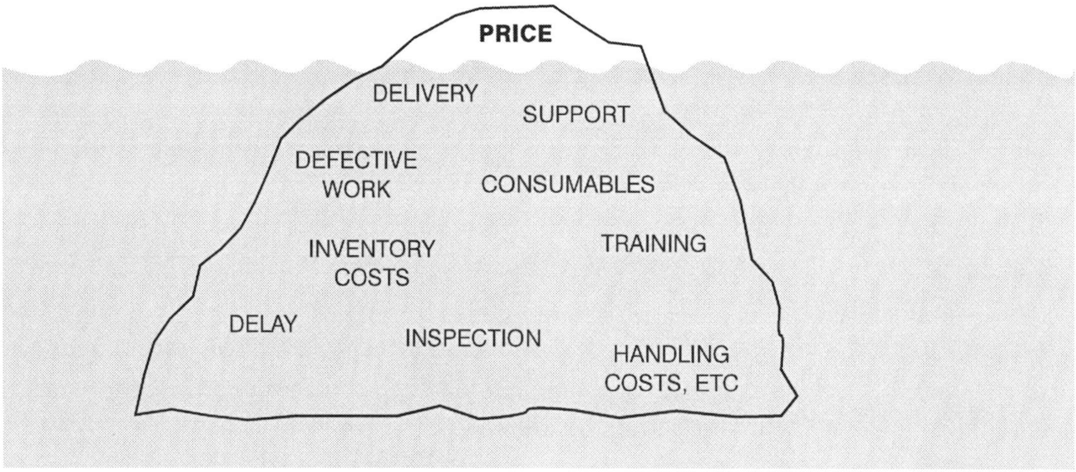

2.13 Some or all of these costs may be included in the price quoted by a supplier, and a purchaser will need to bear this in mind when comparing two quotations: does a lower price reflect competitive pricing – or a lesser total package of benefits?

2.14 More generally, there is a *trade-off* between the purchase price and the total package of benefits. 'It is an obvious fact, yet a commonly ignored one, that a low price may lead to a high total acquisition cost' (Baily *et al*). A lower price may reflect poorer quality, for example, and this will not necessarily be better value for money: the purchase price may be lower, but the total cost of acquisition and ownership may be higher, because of the need for more rigorous quality inspection, the number of rejects and reworks due to poor quality, lost sales through customer disappointment, and so on.

2.15 'Best value' may therefore be defined as the lowest total acquisition cost which meets the purchaser's complex package of requirements (for quality, service, ongoing partnership with the supplier and so on).

2.16 In sum, there is much more to purchasing costs than the basic price charged by the supplier. Important though that is to the 'right price' concept, it is not the whole story...

3 Quality of supplies

Dimensions of product quality

3.1 Quality is, to an extent, 'in the eye of the beholder'. People have different perceptions about what standard of functionality, durability or presentation is 'acceptable' or makes one product 'superior' to another. Some people may associate quality with a premium price, or a brand label. Others will look more closely at whether the product is well designed or made; whether it functions as it should; whether it lasts well; and so on.

3.2 David A Garvin ('Competing in eight dimensions of quality') identifies eight generic dimensions of product quality.

- *Performance*: the operating characteristics of the product
- *Features*: value-adding characteristics and service elements (such as warranties and after-sales service)

- *Reliability*: the ability of the product to perform consistently over time
- *Durability*: the length of time a product will last (and stand up to normal usage) without deterioration or damage
- *Conformance*: whether agreed specifications and standards are met
- *Serviceability*: the ease and availability of service support
- *Aesthetics*: how appealing or pleasing the product is to the senses of the user
- *Perceived quality*: the subjective expectations and perceptions of buyers.

3.3 However, the 'products' of different organisations vary widely – as do the requirements of different types of buyer. 'Quality' will mean something different for a consumer buying clothes than it will for an industrial buyer of clothing material – or industrial safety wear, say. 'Quality' will mean something different for the purchase of computer equipment, engineering components, building materials, cleaning supplies, accountancy services or catering services.

3.4 Definitions of quality have therefore focused on a range of different dimensions.

- *Excellence*: the degree or standard of excellence of a product; the design, workmanship and attention to detail put into it; and the extent to which finished products are free from defects. (Garvin called this the 'transcendent' approach to quality.)
- *Comparative excellence*: how favourably a product is measured against competitive benchmarks (other products), best practice or standards of excellence
- *Quality of design*: the range of potential customer satisfactions built into a product
- *Fitness for purpose or use*: that is, the extent to which a product does what it is designed and expected to do; or, more generally, the extent to which it meets the customer's needs. (Garvin called this the 'user-based' approach to quality.)
- *Conformance to requirement or specification*: that is, the product matches the features, attributes, performance and standards set out in the specification. Conformance therefore also implies lack of defects, and therefore reflects on the quality of the producer's processes. (The 'product-based' or 'manufacturing-based' approach to quality.)
- *Acceptable quality and value for money*: buyers may be willing to sacrifice some performance and features in order to pay a lower price for a product, as long as it is still fit for purpose. (A 'value-based' approach to quality.)

3.5 For a buyer looking to buy materials, components or other supplies in a commercial setting, the most important definitions of 'right quality' are likely to be fitness for purpose and conformance to specification. Note that both of these criteria are essentially focused on the supplier's ability to satisfy the needs and expectations of the customer or buyer. Arjen van Weele argues that: 'Quality is the degree in which customer requirements are met. We speak of a quality product or quality service when supplier and customer agree on requirements and those requirements are met.'

Fitness for purpose

3.6 The British Standards definition of quality is: 'the totality of features and characteristics of a product or service that bear on its ability to satisfy a given need.'

3.7 Fitness for use or purpose was the focus of quality guru **Joseph Juran**, whose work you may come across in your later CIPS studies. It is also one of the key legal definitions of quality, as we see in Section 14 of the (UK) Sale of Goods Act 1979, which states that where a seller supplies goods in the course of a business, he is bound to provide goods:

- Of *satisfactory quality*: working and in good condition (so far as may be reasonably expected) and free from 'minor defects' (unless these are drawn to the buyer's attention or obvious to any reasonable pre-purchase inspection)
- *Fit for the purpose* for which they are commonly used, or for any specific purpose made known by the buyer to the seller.

3.8 So an industrial grinder of the 'right quality' is one that grinds. And if the buyer requested a grinder that would tackle a particular material, and grind it to a specific degree of fineness – that is what it should do. In the same way a bucket of the 'right quality' should hold water – and if the buyer asks for a 5-litre bucket, it should hold up to 5 litres of water.

Specifications and quality

3.9 A specification is simply a statement of the requirements to be satisfied in the supply of a product or service. The role of a specification is to define and communicate the buyer's requirements, in terms of either:

- *Conformance*: the buyer details exactly what the required product, part or material must consist of, and a 'quality' product is one which conforms to the description provided by the buyer – or
- *Performance*: the buyer describes what he expects the part or material to be able to achieve, in terms of the functions it will perform and the level of performance it should reach. A 'quality' product is then one which will satisfy these requirements: the buyer specifies the 'ends' (purpose) and the supplier has relative flexibility about the 'means' of achieving them.

3.10 The specification can then provide a means of evaluating the quality or conformance of the goods or services supplied, for acceptance (if conforming to specification) or rejection (if non-conforming).

3.11 The first step for buyers in securing the 'right quality' will therefore be clear and accurate specification of exactly what is required. Essential though this is, however, conformance to specification is not sufficient to secure 'the right quality'. Indeed, it is possible to envisage a situation in which a product conforms to the buyer's specification (is of 'specified quality') – but doesn't do what it is supposed to do, or doesn't perform efficiently, or is difficult to maintain and operate – and is therefore, arguably, not of 'right quality' overall.

3.12 This is a particular risk if the specification is of the conformance type, because supply quality is measured by the extent to which the supplier has complied with the buyer's description or 'prescription' of the requirement: that is, conformance. If the specification itself is limited, vague, inaccurate, incompatible with other elements of the buyer's processes – or just wrong – the work may conform to specification, but still not be fit for purpose.

3.13 The situation is slightly better with performance specifications, because supply quality is measured by the extent to which the supplied goods are able to do what the buyer asks or expects them to do: that is, fitness for purpose. However, they may still be incompatible with the buyer's true requirements in other ways: difficult or costly to use, say, or incompatible with the buyer's other systems – or perhaps quickly rendered outdated and obsolete by technological change. Again, such goods would arguably not be of the 'right quality' from the buyer's point of view.

Service quality

3.14 Most of what we've said so far about 'product quality' also applies to services – and you should think of 'products' as meaning 'products and/or services'. However, in certain important respects, services are not like products. A service has been defined as 'any activity or benefit that one party can offer to another that is essentially intangible and does not result in the ownership of anything' (Philip Kotler).

3.15 Why are services different when it comes to quality definition and management?

- Because services are intangible, it is much more difficult to specify service requirements accurately, and to measure them, when delivered, against specifications and expectations. You can tell if a widget has the right dimensions, shape and colour. But how do you decide what the 'right' architectural design or security service should look like?
- Because services are produced by different people in unique circumstances each time, it is much more difficult to standardise the quality or consistency of service provision. You can make a machine churn out widgets of standard quality. But how do you make one person in one place and time behave exactly the same as another person in another place and time?
- The exact purpose or use of physical goods will usually be known, and their fitness for purpose can therefore be assessed objectively. It is harder to assess the many factors involved in providing a service: what weight should be placed on the friendliness or smart appearance of the supplier's staff, say, compared with the efficiency with which they get the job done?

4 Timing of supplies

Stockholding policies

4.1 The 'right time' for delivery depends to a large extent on the buying organisation's policies about holding stock.

4.2 On the one hand, it is straightforward to say that goods must be 'on time': that is, not late for a production or delivery deadline. Late delivery deadlines set by a purchaser, or late deliveries by a supplier, may cause the following problems.

- Production 'bottlenecks' and stoppages, as machines or assembly lines wait for required supplies
- Costs associated with idle time (while waiting for delivery) and/or seeking out alternative 'emergency' supplies
- Late delivery of finished goods to the organisation's end customers, with attendant loss of trust, credibility and goodwill (and potentially, therefore, loss of future business), and possibly also late delivery penalties.

4.3 On the other hand, it is not necessarily a good thing for purchasers to set 'early' delivery deadlines (that is, to secure supplies before they are required for use) – because of the costs of holding stock, the risk of obsolescence and deterioration of goods in stock, and the difficulty of accurately forecasting demand in advance. The 'right time' may be 'just in time' for requirement.

4.4 Moreover, as our brief outline of 'just in time' supply suggests, there is an increasing emphasis on 'responsiveness' to customer demand – essentially, a 'time' factor – as an important source of competitive advantage. Organisations that can respond swiftly to customer orders, or to changing environmental factors, by getting hold of supplies at short notice, are able to offer customers leading edge products (because of the speed of getting products to market); swift, flexible service (because of the ability to fill customer orders quickly); and perhaps product customisation (because of the ability to finish or assemble orders to customer specification quickly). The 'right time' may therefore be a matter of supply chain responsiveness or agility: speed and flexibility of action.

Understanding supplier lead times

4.5 The expression 'lead time' has a number of different meanings, and it is important for users and purchasers to understand the true or total length of the lead time to obtain goods, when operating demand management or stock replenishment systems.

- The **internal lead time** is the lead time for the processes carried out within the buying organisation: that is, the time between the identification of a need and the issue of a completed purchase order. This might therefore include the preparation of a specification; the identification and selection of suppliers; contract negotiation and so on.
- The **external lead time** is the lead time for the processes carried out within the supplying organisation: that is, the time between the supplier receiving the purchase order and fulfilling that order (by delivering the goods). It might therefore include process development, manufacture, despatch and delivery time.
- The **total lead time** is therefore a combination of internal and external lead time: that is, the time between the identification of a need by the buyer to delivery of goods by the supplier. As the most comprehensive definition, this is the safest lead time to use in planning to obtain goods at the 'right time'.

5 Quantity and place of supplies

The right quantity

5.1 What is the 'right quantity' to buy in a given situation? Of course, it varies. If you receive a requisition from the operations manager to replace one worn lathe, say, the 'right quantity' is one. If a bill of materials for a customer order specifies 2,000 subassemblies, the 'right quantity' is 2,000 subassemblies. But what if your company produces cars: how many components will it need in a given period? How much oil will it need to lubricate its assembly line? How much toilet paper will it need for the factory and offices? And what if you receive that requisition for one lathe – but you know that another lathe will become worn out shortly: is it more advantageous to buy one lathe now, or two? Buyers will have to work with users and inventory managers to establish the optimum quantity (and timing) of purchases for a given situation.

5.2 Lysons & Farrington suggest that the most important factors determining the 'right quantity' to purchase in a given situation are as follows.

- *Demand for the final product* into which the purchased materials and components are incorporated (dependent demand). Obviously, the more cars you anticipate selling, the more wheels you are going to have to buy – and if you are planning on producing 1,000 cars in a given period, you will need 4,000 wheels in the same period.
- *Demand for purchased finished items*, such as office equipment and supplies, computer hardware and software or maintenance services (independent demand). This may be based on past and average usage and replacement rates, for example. If your office gets through an average of 60 reams of paper per month, you will probably plan to purchase a similar quantity on a monthly basis.

- *The inventory policy of the organisation*: whether its main aim is to secure service levels by holding stocks (as a 'buffer' against unforeseen demand or supply difficulties) – or to minimise or eliminate stocks, to avoid the costs and risks associated with holding stock
- *The service level required*: whether an item must be available in full on demand 100% of the time (eg for critical production items or hospital supplies) or only 90–95% of the time (eg for routine supplies)
- *Market conditions*, affecting the price and security of supply, which dictate whether requirements must be 'stockpiled' to secure supply or take advantage of low prices, or can be bought on an *ad hoc* or opportunistic basis
- *Supply-side factors*, such as minimum order quantities or values, or price incentives for bulk purchases
- *Factors determining the economic order quantity (EOQ)* which balances the costs of acquiring stock (higher with frequent smaller orders) against the costs of holding stock (higher with fewer larger orders)
- *Specific quantities notified to buyers by user departments, according to identified needs.* For example, the operations function may indicate required quantities for a particular job or application via materials specifications or a bill of materials (BOM). Standard items, consumables and spares may be ordered by purchase requisitions from user departments or stock control staff. Computerised inventory reports (or the electronic point of sale systems in a retail organisation) may specify re-order quantities when inventory gets down to a predetermined level, in order to 'top up' stock in line with anticipated demand.

4

The right place

5.3 You might think the 'right place' is fairly obvious: as long as you've given your supplier the right address, how complicated could it be? The fact is that deliveries do go astray for various reasons, and buyers must take care to ensure that there is no misunderstanding about the delivery address. But there are many other issues involved in deciding 'the right place'.

5.4 Do you ask the supplier to make deliveries directly to a number of different user sites (factories, branch offices or retail outlets, say), or to make a single delivery to a regional distribution centre, which will distribute them as required?

5.5 What kind of transport will you ask the supplier to use, or arrange yourself, in order to ensure that the goods get to the right place (at the right time, safely and in good condition), with minimal cost and impact on the environment? How should the goods be packaged for this mode of transport?

5.6 Many of these decisions will already have been made. The organisation will either have a regional distribution centre, or use a third party logistics provider, or it won't. There may be company policies about the use of particular transport modes and packaging for different types of delivery. There will be existing procedures – and legal requirements – for preparing the relevant documentation. Nevertheless, buyers need to understand the basis on which these decisions are made.

Specifying delivery

5.7 A number of different considerations are thus important in defining delivery to 'the right place' (by the right means). Each of the following points should be covered in the purchase order, delivery specification or contract with a supplier.

- A full and accurate delivery address (with as much detail as possible to ensure that the driver can find the delivery point easily: eg if there is an unloading bay number)
- The contact person at the delivery address, who will have been informed of the incoming delivery and will be authorised to inspect and sign for it
- Packaging instructions (eg if goods require refrigeration or special handling for preservation, safety or security reasons; or if goods need to be packaged ready for handling or storage)
- Delivery instructions (eg if there is a defined schedule or 'window' of opportunity for deliveries, while a delivery bay is open, staffed and/or available; or if there are restrictions on the size of vehicle that can access the delivery point)
- Transport instructions, if the contract includes a particular type, speed or cost of transport (eg air, sea or rail freight)
- The point at which ownership or title in the goods (and therefore all risks and liabilities associated with them) 'pass' from the supplier to the buyer: this may be at any stage in the journey from supplier to buyer. Where the time in transit is lengthy and prone to risk, as in international deliveries, it is very important that the liability for risk (and insurance) is clearly established.

6 Value for money

6.1 Obtaining value for money means not paying too much for the total package of value (quality and service) you are getting. It also, perhaps more surprisingly, means not paying too little: a very low price may reflect a supplier's desire to win your business – but it may also result in corner cutting on quality somewhere along the line.

6.2 There is frequently a trade-off between cost objectives and objectives relating to quality, service and delivery. This has led to the recognition that cost/price and 'value' are not the same thing. 'Value for money' is an important strategic objective, particularly in the public and non-profit sector. It may be defined as 'the optimum combination of whole life cost and the quality necessary to meet the customer's requirement'.

6.3 Value for money must also be measured in relation to the resources or opportunities that must be given up in order to obtain it. A rough idea of value for money – not a formal definition – can be given by the concept of a ratio: the ratio of benefit obtained compared to cash or other resources expended in order to achieve it.

6.4 You should refer back to Chapter 2 for a fuller discussion of value for money.

Chapter summary

- The five rights of purchasing are inputs of the right quality, delivered in the right quantity, to the right place, at the right time, and for the right price. There are often trade-offs between the five rights.
- The right price does not necessarily mean the lowest possible price. Buyers seek value for money – a good price consistent with other objectives, such as satisfactory quality.
- Initial purchase price is only one element of the total cost of ownership or total acquisition cost. In many cases, a low purchase price may lead to a higher than necessary total cost of ownership.
- There are many definitions of the right quality but fitness for purpose and conformance to specification are two of the important criteria for assessing it.
- Ensuring the right time for delivery involves an understanding of supplier lead times.
- The right quantity is closely bound up with the right place.

Self-test questions

Numbers in brackets refer to the paragraphs where you can check your answers.

1 List the five rights of purchasing. (1.1)

2 Apart from the five rights, what other objectives may purchasing need to pursue? (1.5)

3 List some of the possible trade-offs between the five rights. (1.7)

4 Distinguish between price and value for money. (2.4)

5 Apart from purchase price, what other elements may be included in total cost of ownership? (2.11)

6 List some of the possible dimensions along which quality may be assessed. (3.2, 3.4)

7 How can a specification assist in evaluating quality? (3.9)

8 What is meant by internal lead time and external lead time? (4.5)

9 List possible factors in determining the right quantity to purchase. (5.2)

10 Suggest details that might be included when specifying delivery to 'the right place'. (5.7)

CHAPTER 5

Delivering Products to Customers

Assessment criteria and indicative content

2.1 Describe the delivery of products and services that organisations make to customers

- Defining products and services
- The customer role
- Seeing customers as a part of a supply chain

Section headings

1 Defining products and services
2 Special features of services
3 The role of the customer

1 Defining products and services

Suppliers and customers

1.1 As we have seen, supply chains consist of organisations linked to each other with a view to providing products to end users. (We use the term 'products', as is common, to include both tangible products and intangible services.) A typical organisation within a supply chain is both a customer (purchasing from its suppliers the materials and services it needs in order to conduct its business), and a supplier (selling its finished products to customers further along the chain).

1.2 The focus of this chapter is on the delivery of products to customers. In other words, we are looking at organisations primarily as suppliers of goods and services. This may seem strange to you – after all, you are training to be a buyer, not a supplier. However, as we will see, many aspects of a purchaser's work have an important influence on the products and services that his organisation can supply to customers.

Categories of supply

1.3 We begin by identifying different categories of supply. The reason for this is that approaches to buying and selling may differ depending on what exactly is being bought and sold. As a starting point we distinguish between direct and indirect supplies.

- *Direct supplies* – items that form part of the end product of an organisation. For a manufacturing organisation, direct supplies are the raw materials and components that will be assembled to form the end product.

  For a retail organisation, direct supplies are the products bought for onward sale to customers. Many of these goods may be held in warehouses and delivered to the shops as required but some may be delivered directly to the store or even directly to the customer.

  Direct supplies are critical to the success of organisations so it is essential that the purchasing process is efficient and achieves the five rights on every occasion.

- *Indirect supplies* – products that an organisation uses internally, such as stationery. For service organisations, most purchases will be in this category. Indirect supplies are often perceived to be less important than direct supplies. This is not the case. Indirect supplies allow the organisation to carry out its main role and should be considered just as important as direct supplies.

1.4 In principle, all supplies can be placed into one or other of these categories although the line may become blurred. For example, a shop might buy stationery to sell to its customers and also to use internally.

1.5 An alternative and overlapping classification is to divide supplies according to how they are used within an organisation.

- *Maintenance, repair and operations (MRO) supplies*. This is a special category of indirect supply which covers the spare parts and other goods required to maintain the machinery within an organisation. All machinery, lifting gear, conveyors, etc require servicing on a regular preventive cycle. The servicing schedule will attempt to reduce the impact of servicing on the production schedule. If the required goods aren't purchased in line with the servicing schedule the manufacturing process might be disrupted.
- *Services*. Services can be direct – such as galvanising steel parts for the end product of a manufacturer – or indirect – such as cleaning or accountancy services. Most indirect service supplies will be acquired through medium to long-term contracts because this gives stability and allows the supplier to improve his service as the relationship develops. A service is intangible and at the end of the transaction nothing has changed ownership. A client pays for a solicitor's legal opinion but he doesn't own that opinion and the solicitor is free to sell the same opinion to someone else with the same problem. Purchasing services often requires a more formal process than purchasing products and will usually involve a written contract.
- *Capital equipment*. This equipment becomes part of the assets of the organisation. It is called capital equipment because it may use a large amount of capital to buy. It tends to be large, expensive and bought on a one-off basis. Examples might be a lathe, a van, a forklift truck, a mainframe computer, or an office or factory building. Because this equipment is bought at irregular intervals it is best to think of it as a completely new purchase every time. If a forklift truck is replaced every five years so much will have changed since the last purchase that the research into suppliers will need to be done again.

Contrasting products and services

1.6 Buying services is usually more difficult than buying products. This is because of the difficulty in specifying exactly what we want. An example might be defining what is meant by 'clean' in an office cleaning contract. Does it mean swept, dusted, washed or scrubbed? Who is to judge whether the floor is 'clean' at the end of the scrubbing process?

1.7 The peculiar characteristics of services have been much discussed, in the marketing literature as much as in standard purchasing texts. For example, marketing texts frequently refer to intangibility, inseparability, variability, perishability, and lack of ownership as features which distinguish services from physical products. Mirroring this from the purchasing viewpoint, Baily, Farmer, Jessop and Jones in *Purchasing Principles and Management* refer to impracticability of storage, lack of 'inspectability', uncertainties in contractual arrangements, and sheer complexity.

1.8 Table 5.1 lists some of these points (and others).

Table 5.1 *Characteristics of goods and services*

GOODS	SERVICES
Tangible	Intangible
Can be inventoried	Cannot be inventoried
Little customer contact	Extensive customer contact
Standard customer contact	Flexible customer contact
Long lead times	Short lead times
Capital intensive	Labour intensive
Quality easy to assess	Quality very difficult to assess

Products and services: a marketing perspective

1.9 We begin by looking at the marketing perspective.

1.10 **Intangibility** refers to the lack of substance that is involved in service delivery. Unlike goods there are no physical aspects, no taste, no feel etc. This can inhibit the choice of a customer to use a service, as they are not sure what they will receive.

1.11 **Inseparability**. A service often cannot be separated from the provider of the service. The creation or the performance often occurs at the same instant that a full or partial consumption of it occurs. Goods must be produced, then sold, then consumed (in that order). Services are only a promise at the time they are sold; most services are sold and then are produced and consumed simultaneously.

1.12 **Variability (heterogeneity)**. Many services face a problem of maintaining consistency in the standard of output. Variability of quality in delivery is inevitable because of the number of factors that can influence it. It may prove difficult or impossible either to attain precise standardisation of the service offered or to influence or control perceptions of what is good or bad customer service.

5

1.13 **Perishability**. Services cannot be stored. Seats at a concert, provision of a lecture, services of a dentist, consist of their availability for periods of time. Perishability presents specific marketing problems. Meeting customer needs in these operations depends on staff being available as and when they are needed. This must be balanced against the need for a firm to minimise unnecessary expenditure on staff wages. Anticipating and responding to levels of demand is a key planning priority.

1.14 **Lack of ownership**. Services differ fundamentally from goods in that purchase does not result in a transfer of property. The purchase of a service only confers on the customer access to or rights to use a facility – not ownership. This may lower the customer's perception of the service's value.

1.15 These kinds of challenges present a strong argument for purchasing to be involved in sourcing services – rather than users, who may lack expertise in demand forecasting, negotiation, specification, contracting and ongoing supplier management.

Products and services: a buyer's perspective

1.16 The above factors can to some extent be mirrored by looking at the buyer's perspective on services as opposed to physical goods. We adopt the features identified as distinctive by *Baily et al.*

1.17 **Impracticability of storage**. This can give rise to scheduling problems, and the effect of this is that the purchase of services is typically the subject of detailed forward planning between buyer and supplier. Of course, the difficulty does not apply to all services: *Baily et al* cite cleaning services, which are usually not time-critical, and insurance, which is usually provided continuously in return for an annual premium.

1.18 **Lack of inspectability**. A service cannot be measured, weighed or chemically analysed to check compliance with specification. Indeed the whole issue of specifying service levels is full of difficulty, and many of the problems that commonly arise spring from disagreement between buyer and supplier as to what was agreed.

1.19 **Uncertainties in contractual agreements**. This is another aspect of the specification problem. *Baily et al* cite the case of an architect who submits a design meeting the criteria of the client in terms of budget, required accommodation etc; and yet the client finds the design unsatisfying on aesthetic grounds. Who, if anyone, is at fault and who pays for the architect's second attempt?

1.20 **Complexity**. The purchase of a tangible asset **sometimes** involves the purchase of a service; for example, if you purchase a large item of machinery, the manufacturer may provide your staff with training on its use. But the converse is **nearly always** true: most service providers will also have to supply tangible product along with the service. For example, a training organisation will invariably provide delegates to its courses with course handouts. This mix of product and service elements adds to the complexity facing the purchaser.

1.21 Still, among all this discussion of the distinctive nature of services it is easy to forget that there are also essential similarities between services and tangible products.

- Services can be specified and costed.
- Services can be measured and assessed.
- Service suppliers can be rated and assessed.
- Services can be segmented in ways that help purchasers to analyse them.

The mix of products and services

1.22 The products supplied by a business may be either goods or services or a mix of the two. The proportions of goods and services in the mix will vary from industry to industry. Table 5.2 gives some hypothetical examples (with percentages included for illustration only).

Table 5.2 *The mix of goods and services supplied by different industries*

OPERATION	GOODS	SERVICES
Mining	95%	5%
Vending machines	95%	5%
Low-cost consumable goods	80%	20%
Home computers	75%	25%
Fast-food operation	60%	40%
High-quality restaurant meal	30%	70%
Car breakdown service	25%	75%
Local authority	25%	75%
Teaching	5%	95%

1.23 We can elaborate on some of the examples from Table 5.2.

- With mining the purpose is to extract raw materials. Little emphasis is placed on the delivery of support services with the exception of transportation to a port or for refinement.
- A fast-food restaurant offers a mix of a limited product range with a standardised approach to service; a more upmarket restaurant provides better facilities and specialised advice; a local authority provides goods (eg the books and magazines in a library), but concentrates more on offering a range of support services that meet the needs of the community (in terms of refuse collection, street cleaning etc).

1.24 This analysis demonstrates that most operations produce a mix of goods and services.

1.25 In recent years we have seen major changes in two key areas that affect the mix of goods and services supplied.

- **Customer service requirements**. Customers are becoming more demanding and require better and consistently high levels of customer service. One approach is to use this to the supplier's benefit and 'add value' to the customer experience. Delivery in 24 hours, late product customisation, 'delighting' the customer with unexpected upgrades and improvements at no extra cost, are all examples. The reward can be better customer relationships and retention, leading to an improvement in the operation overall.
- **The impact of information technology**. Information and communication technologies can allow for the provision and standardisation of services in a way that can be easily understood by customers. A well designed website can provide company information, product information and purchase information together with a secure method of purchase and detail on subsequent delivery.

2 Special features of services

Categorising services

2.1 As we saw in an earlier chapter, services have been defined by Kotler as: 'any activity of benefit that one party can offer to another that is essentially intangible and does not result in the ownership of anything. Its production may or may not be tied to a physical product'.

2.2 Carla S Lallatin categorises the services most commonly used by organisations: Figure 5.1.

Figure 5.1 *Lallatin's categorisation of services*

TYPES OF SERVICES				
Personal	**Professional**	**Support**	**Personnel**	**Construction**
Technical editing *Translation* *Appraisals*	*Management and other consultants* *Legal services* *Medical services* *Insurance services*	*Administrative* *Financial* *Information management* *Procurement and logistics services* *Waste management*	*Recruitment and selection* *Training and development* *Welfare services*	*Building repair* *Alteration* *Restoration* *Maintenance services*

2.3 Services involve a higher degree of customer contact and presentation than with the selling of a product. The physical delivery of a service is less of a problem as the service element is intangible.

However, other areas take on a more important role.

- **People**: have a crucial role in providing service. Customer satisfaction can often depend on the person providing the service, because the service is inseparable from the person delivering it. As a result, there is an increased emphasis on staff training and development.
- **Physical evidence**: the ambience surrounding the service being provided. As an example the ambience surrounding a top hotel may serve to convey the nature of the product, reinforce the image of the hotel, engender rapport, imply qualities and transmit messages.
- **Process**: this refers to the methods used to provide the service and is directly related to the role of operations management. Procedures for dealing with customers and for supplying the service must be carefully planned and managed so as to reduce variability.

Quality issues in service delivery

2.4 Quality is key to service delivery. Only the customer can judge quality.

2.5 Quality of service is an increasingly important performance measurement tool in both the public and private sectors. With the move to a more service-orientated economy and greater transparency and accountability being expected in the public sector, the area of service is increasingly being placed under scrutiny.

2.6 Quality of service to customers is, by its nature, subjective and qualitative. Gathering the information provides greater challenges than would be the case with a product, where measures such as rejection rates or percentage for scrap could be used. Questionnaires are commonly used (either by mail, email or over the telephone), although the response rate can be low.

Service level agreements

2.7 A good specification is a vital step in assuring the quality of the eventual service delivery. A Parasuraman lists the following quality characteristics of services.

- Reliability, ie how consistently and dependably the supplier provides the service
- Responsiveness, ie how promptly and willingly supplier staff provide the service
- Competence, ie how skilfully and knowledgeably supplier staff provide the service
- Access, ie how easy it is to access the supplier
- Courtesy, ie how polite the supplier staff are
- Communication, ie how often and how understandably the supplier keeps the customer informed
- Credibility, ie how trustworthy the supplier is
- Security, ie how safe the customer can feel in terms of avoiding risk or danger
- Understanding, ie how hard the supplier works to understand his customer's requirements
- Tangibles, ie the physical goods supplied as part of the service

2.8 A crucial element in the success of external service provision is to reach clear agreement on the level of service to be provided, by means of a service level agreement (SLA). For example, suppose a company decides to hire external contractors to provide office cleaning services. Among the many points to discuss the following basic service level issues should be considered.

- How often is the service to be provided?
- During what hours will the service be carried out, and in particular will there be any disruption to office activities?
- How many staff (and, if relevant, what grades of staff) will be involved in providing the service?

- How far will the service extend (eg does it include cleaning of computer monitors, telephone equipment, etc)?
- What qualifications are needed by staff members providing the service?
- What speed of response is expected from the supplier when the customer makes a request?
- What dispute procedures will be required?

2.9 Speed of response is a major consideration in many types of service provision. This must be carefully considered and agreed when service levels are discussed. It is easy for the purchasing organisation to complain that the service provider is not reacting quickly enough, but the supplier may retort that constant calls for 'urgent' attention suggest lack of forward planning by the purchaser. To avoid this kind of argument both sides must accept a responsibility for planning and communication, as well as agreeing the extent to which the supplier will be required to respond within a particular timescale.

3 The role of the customer

Upstream and downstream activity

3.1 We have already emphasised that most organisations are both buyers (customers) and sellers (suppliers). It is common to refer to upstream and downstream elements of a supply chain. The metaphor pictures a flow of goods downwards from an original supplier to his customer, who in turn supplies his customers and so on. We refer to organisations earlier in the chain than ourselves (ie our suppliers and their suppliers) as being upstream of us; while our customers (and their customers etc) are downstream of us. You should remember this terminology from Chapter 1.

3.2 Upstream and downstream activity includes relationships with intermediary customers, such as distributors and retailers, who in turn supply end customers.

3.3 In principle, every activity and function in an organisation is ultimately directed towards satisfying its customers. That's how it maintains demand for its goods and services, and therefore – in the business sector – how it maintains profitability and competitive advantage. The aim of effective supply chains, both external and internal, is to add value for the customer – and hence, for the organisation.

3.4 We also saw in an earlier chapter that it is possible to envisage a supply chain operating *within* a single organisation (an **internal supply chain**). We will return to this concept later in this chapter, but for now we will concentrate on the links *between* different organisations – ie we will look first at external customers.

Who are your external customers?

3.5 The kinds of external customers an organisation has will depend on its position in the supply chain (the sequence of people and organisations involved in bringing a product or service to its end user from its most basic ingredients), and the sector in which it operates.

3.6 Manufacturing and service firms may distribute products and services direct to end users (whether consumers or other businesses), or they may choose from a wide range of intermediaries or 'middle men': wholesalers, dealers, agents, franchise outlets, retail outlets and so on. The term 'distribution channel' refers to the full set of intermediaries involved in getting goods from the manufacturer to the consumer.

- **Wholesalers** stock a range of products from different manufacturers, to sell on to other organisations, such as retailers. They get discounts from manufacturers for buying in bulk, then 'break bulk' (enabling retailers to buy smaller quantities) at a marked-up price, allowing them to make a profit.
- **Distributors and dealers** contract to buy a manufacturer's goods and sell them to customers: they may offer the product of only one manufacturer (as in the case of car dealerships, for example). In addition to selling, they may also promote the products and provide after-sales service.
- **Agents** do not purchase and resell goods at a profit, but sell goods *on behalf of* the manufacturer, earning a commission on the sale (eg insurance brokers).
- **Franchisees** are independent small businesses which, in exchange for an initial fee (and usually a share of sales revenue) are allowed to trade under the name of the franchise brand. Examples include McDonald's fast food restaurants.
- **Retailers** stock a range of products and sell on to consumers.

3.7 Channel intermediaries perform certain key functions which the producer may not wish to perform, or would be inefficient at performing, itself. Marketing guru Philip Kotler identifies these as follows.

- *Information*. Intermediaries have access to valuable information, gleaned from direct contact with customers, competitors and other players in the market, which can be used for product development planning, demand forecasting, production and materials planning, marketing planning and so on. This may be particularly valuable in international markets, where local distributors may have the key advantage of local knowledge.
- *Promotion and display*. Intermediaries may develop their own promotions to attract customers, and may also promote particular products (often in collaboration with the producer). Retailers, franchises and dealerships also display products at the point of sale.
- *Negotiation.* Intermediaries may negotiate prices and offerings with customers.
- *Ordering.* Intermediaries forecast demand and order on behalf of their own channel or end customers. This can enable efficiencies (such as breaking bulk) or inefficiencies (such as poor demand forecasting and over-ordering leading to over-production and waste).
- *Risk taking.* By paying for the purchase and promotion of products, intermediaries share the risk of not selling the goods onwards.
- *Inventory.* Intermediaries often hold a certain level of stock of finished items, to cover anticipated sales volumes. This can be a vital cost saving for the producer.

3.8 Some of the distribution channel options are illustrated in Figure 5.2.

Figure 5.2 *Distribution channels*

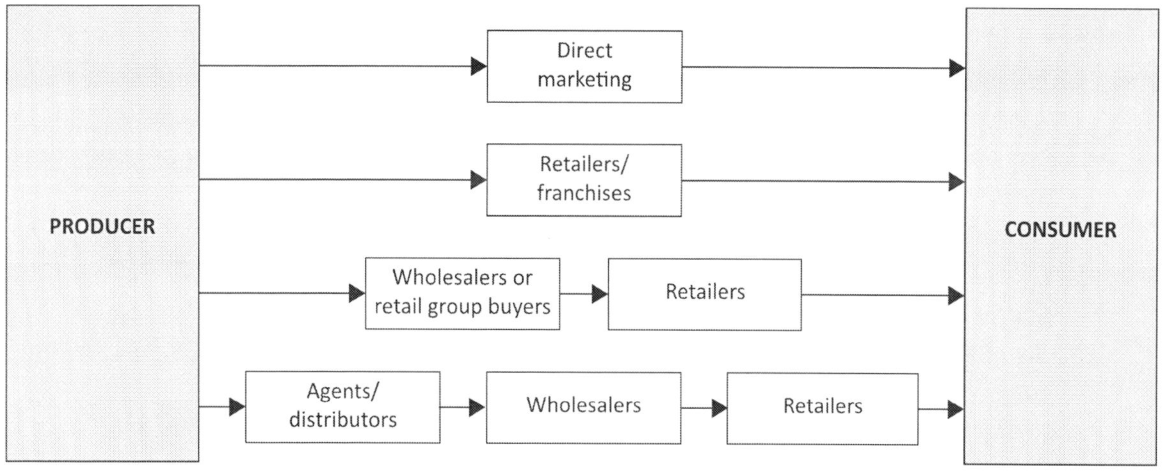

3.9 It is also important to distinguish different types of end-customers.

3.10 *Consumer* markets (eg for household goods, clothing, food and entertainment products) operate quite differently from *industrial, business-to-business* markets (eg for business services, manufacturing components and consumables and so on). (You may sometimes see the terminology B2C markets – ie business to consumer – and B2B markets – ie business to business.)

- Business customers tend to be fewer in number, but purchase at higher volumes and values than consumers.
- Their needs are generally more specialised and complex, and their buying more professional: they will often seek to negotiate a total offering, based on added value elements such as customisation, after-sales service, training and support, life-time costs, relationship with the supplier and so on.
- Because of this, industrial buyer-supplier relationships tend to be more long-term and partnership-oriented than consumer relationships, which tend to be more opportunistic, based on competing promotions and offers, with greater ease of switching from one brand and supplier to another.

3.11 In the *not-for-profit and public sectors*, it is important to remember that charities, schools and universities, museums, trade unions, hospitals, sports centres and so on still have 'customers' – target audiences or beneficiaries – of some kind.

3.12 The buyer's role in an organisation may also differ considerably, according to who its external customers are. Buyers in a retail organisation, for example, select and buy the products which they think consumers will want to buy. They need to be much closer to consumer preferences and trends, almost in a marketing role. Buyers in a manufacturing organisation are more focused on specification of the products and services required by the manufacturing process.

Characteristics of external customer relationships

3.13 Despite the differences between external customer groups, we can still observe some general characteristics of external customer relationships.

- External customers often have a considerable choice of suppliers, and freedom to switch suppliers as they wish. There may be some 'inertia' or slowness to switch suppliers in B2B markets where buyers and suppliers establish partnerships, but consumer markets are notoriously fickle (and, research suggests, increasingly so). This means that suppliers are in competition to attract and retain customers, placing a premium on strategies for customer satisfaction, customer retention and customer loyalty. This is the case for not-for-profit organisations, too: a charity, for example, may compete for voluntary labour and donations not only with other charitable causes but with a host of other uses for people's time and money.

- External customers have objectives and agendas of their own from buying products and services, and marketing organisations must take these into account. They cannot rely on goodwill to retain customers who can get a better deal or experience elsewhere. There may be fundamental conflicts of interest over price, for example, particularly for business customers who have their own profitability to consider.
- External customers have commercial (and therefore enforceable) contracts with suppliers. Their rights are protected by contract and consumer protection law, in areas such as product safety, accurate product descriptions in advertising, the right to refuse or return goods of unsatisfactory quality and so on.
- External customers generally pay a commercial rate or price for the goods and services they receive. They are therefore likely to be demanding in terms of value for money, and sensitive to price competition (although some markets are more price sensitive than others).
- External customers may not be easy to identify or reach personally – especially in mass consumer markets. The organisation will have to put effort into researching the market, segmenting it (identifying component groups whose needs and preferences can be more accurately targeted), gaining access to it (by advertising in relevant media, obtaining relevant mailing lists and so on) and, where possible, communicating with it in a more personal, relationship-building way (eg by permission-based email marketing, personalised web content, loyalty scheme memberships and so on).

Who are your internal customers?

3.14 The internal customer concept implies that any unit of the organisation whose task contributes to the task of other units (whether as part of a process, or in an advisory, support or service relationship) can be regarded as a supplier of goods and services like any other supplier: each link in the value chain is a customer of the one before. Looked at this way, the objective of each unit is the efficient and effective identification and satisfaction of the needs and wants of its internal customers or clients.

3.15 This is a constructive way of looking at internal relationships, because it helps to integrate the objectives of different units throughout the value chain. It focuses on the process of adding value for the ultimate customer (rather than the separate goals and methods of each unit or function); and it makes each unit look carefully at what added value it is able to offer.

3.16 As a service function and an internal consultancy, the purchasing function has many different customers and clients in the organisation. They may include the following.

- Senior management, who expect their strategic objectives to be met through effective procurement and supply chain management
- Related functions in the internal supply chain, such as finance, engineering, manufacturing, warehousing and logistics, which depend on co-ordination with purchasing to secure the efficient flow of information and goods into, through and out of the organisation

- Managers in 'user' functions, on whose behalf purchasers procure goods and services, and who expect timely supply of the right quality and quantity of resources to meet their own objectives. Most obviously, this would include the production function in a manufacturing organisation, for whose processes purchasers procure raw materials, components and consumables. However, purchasing may also procure computer hardware for the finance department, advertising agency services for the marketing department, cleaning supplies for maintenance, office supplies for general use – and so on.
- Staff in other functions who carry out some purchasing for their own units (sometimes called 'part–time purchasers'), and who may need advice and/or assistance from purchasing specialists: help with requisitioning, product specification, contracting or supplier management; advice on negotiation; and/or information on market prices or sources of supply, say.

Characteristics of internal customer relationships

3.17 It can be a complex business having customers or clients within your own organisation. Internal customer relationships are different from external buyer-supplier relationships in several key respects.

- Internal customers will often not have a legal 'contract for services', or even an explicit agreement on service requirements and standards, with internal service suppliers. Relationships are more often negotiated and based on over-arching corporate objectives and departmental performance measures. There is a risk that mutual expectations will not be clearly stated, creating potential for misunderstanding and conflict.
- There may not be a direct fee or charge levied for the internal provider's services, although the cost of the service will usually be accounted for in some way. This may raise questions about what level of service internal customers are entitled to demand ('you get what you pay for') – and what the service department gets in return for its services: where is the 'exchange' or reciprocity in the relationship, which is a feature of external marketing transactions?
- Internal customers do not generally have the choice to choose or switch suppliers – although it should be noted that purchasing (among other internal activities) can be outsourced to external service providers. This lack of competition may pose a challenge for maintaining service levels, but it also enables a high degree of integration and trust to be developed over time.
- Usually, internal customers are personally known to internal suppliers, and there will be established channels for communication, information sharing and collaboration. Even so, purchasing may have to put some effort into developing internal contacts and networks, and into marketing itself within the organisation.
- There may be conflicts and differences of interest between functions. Staff or service functions are often perceived as overly bureaucratic and 'interfering' in the more directly value-adding line functions such as production and sales, for example. Different functions will have their own priorities and objectives.
- In general, however – and unlike external buyer-supplier relations – the goals and objectives of internal customers and suppliers are (or should be) broadly shared or aligned, in the overall interest of the firm.

3.18 Nevertheless, in most respects an internal customer should be treated as any external customer should be treated: the aim is to deliver a product or service that meets the customer's needs and expectations.

Chapter summary

- Supplies may be categorised as direct or indirect; or they may be classified by how they are used (MRO supplies, services, capital equipment etc).
- Services have features that do not apply to tangible products. The overall effect of this is that services are typically more difficult to specify and source.
- Most organisations supply a mix of tangible products and services.
- When purchasing a service, it is normal to specify service level agreements, defining the level of service expected from the supplier.
- Buyers deal with both internal and external customers and suppliers. In relation to customers, there are important differences in the characteristics of internal and external customers.

Self-test questions

Numbers in brackets refer to the paragraphs where you can check your answers.

1 Distinguish between direct and indirect supplies. (1.3)

2 What is meant by MRO supplies? (1.5)

3 From a marketing perspective, what are the characteristics that distinguish services from tangible products? (1.10ff)

4 From a buyer's perspective, what are the characteristics that distinguish services from tangible products? (1.17ff)

5 What categories of service are distinguished by Carla Lallatin? (2.2)

6 List the quality characteristics of services identified by A Parasuruman. (2.7)

7 Suggest items that might be included in a service level agreement for an office cleaning contract. (2.8)

8 List organisations that might form part of a distribution channel. (3.6)

9 Distinguish between B2B and B2C markets. (3.10)

10 List general characteristics of relationships with external customers. (3.13)

CHAPTER 6

Delivery of Products by Suppliers

Assessment criteria and indicative content

2.2 Describe the delivery of products and services made by external suppliers

- The need for supplies of products and services from external suppliers
- Outsourced services
- Seeing suppliers as a part of a supply chain

Section headings

1 The need for external supplies
2 The outsourcing decision
3 Outsourcing in practice

1 The need for external supplies

Why buy from external suppliers?

1.1 In theory, it might be possible to imagine an organisation that needs no supplies from outside. At the time of writing (March 2012) there is an advertisement on UK television which shows a young girl selling cups of cool drinks to passers by from a table set up outside her front garden. Clearly her need for external resources is very limited, but even this little entrepreneur needs somehow to acquire water, fruit juice concentrate, plastic cups etc.

1.2 In a more realistic scenario it is clear that very many resources required by an organisation cannot sensibly be acquired unless from external suppliers. Consider a government department, for example, operating from a large office building.

- It is inconceivable that this organisation will generate its own utility services: its own electricity supply, its own water supply, its own telecommunication networks. It must be cheaper and more convenient to buy from established utilities companies.
- Equally, the department cannot feasibly create its own stationery supplies – setting up a manufacturing department to create paper, ink cartridges, pens and pencils, storage files etc. Again, it must be cheaper and more convenient to buy from one of the numerous specialist stationery suppliers.
- And in recent years, such departments have shown greater readiness to purchase even products and services that might once have been provided from internal resources. For example, many organisations that used to employ in-house cleaners no longer do so, and instead buy in cleaning services from external specialists.

1.3 A key issue that organisations have faced in recent years is exactly where to draw the line. Exactly where do we establish the boundaries of the firm? Exactly which supplies do we produce from our own internal resources and which do we buy from external suppliers? This is one of the key themes of the present chapter. But it should be clear from the examples already given that no organisation realistically can decide to 'go it alone' for all of the supplies it needs. Even the smallest organisation will have to buy some of its requirements from external suppliers.

1.4 This dilemma about 'where to draw the line' is sometimes referred to as the 'make/do or buy' decision or simply the 'make-or-buy' decision. In other words, what products do we make ourselves and what services do we do ourselves, and on the other hand what products and services do we buy in from others?

1.5 The nature of the make/do or buy problem can be stated in fairly simple terms. At one extreme, a manufacturing firm (for example) could make its products almost entirely in-house, buying in perhaps nothing but raw materials. The value of the final product arises almost entirely from the work done by the firm.

- Raw material extraction
- Design
- Manufacture
- Assembly
- Distribution

1.6 At the other extreme, a firm could minimise its own activities, buying in almost everything from outside suppliers or subcontractors (who would therefore be adding almost all the value in the finished product).

1.7 It is a matter of corporate policy to determine the answer to this question. Control of all the factors listed under the bullet points above offers two main advantages.

- By having everything under central control the objective is to improve reliability and responsiveness. However, organisations that attempt to do this often prove to be too cumbersome and bureaucratic to be effectively managed and are rarely found in practice. The absence of competition can also lead to deterioration in service and quality.
- As external providers need to make a profit it is assumed they will be more expensive. However, this is not necessarily so: a supplier specialising exclusively in one type of activity may be able to produce outputs more efficiently (and cheaply) than an organisation for which this supply is not a particular competency.

Organisational competencies

1.8 In most cases, of course, firms will occupy a middle position somewhere between the two extremes. They will make/do some things themselves, and buy in other things from external suppliers. One consideration that helps to determine where to draw the line is the issue of organisational competency – the fact that a particular organisation is good at certain things, but has no particular specialism (or competency) in other things.

1.9 Competencies are 'the activities or processes through which the organisation deploys its resources effectively' *(Johnson, Scholes and Whittington)*.

1.10 **Threshold** competencies are the basic capabilities necessary to support a particular strategy or to enable the organisation to compete in a given market. (The effective use of IT systems would now be considered a threshold competency in most markets.)

1.11 **Core** competencies are distinctive value-creating skills, capabilities and resources. They offer sustainable competitive advantage: for example by enabling differentiation or cost leadership, or putting up barriers to competitor entry into an industry.

1.12 *Hamel and Prahalad* argue that 'senior managers must conceive of their companies as a portfolio of core competencies, rather than just a portfolio of businesses and products'.

1.13 The idea of **outsourcing** non-core activities (ie buying in goods and services for which the organisation has no particular competency) has been a key argument of Prahalad and Hamel. They believe that organisations should manage and leverage their **core competencies** to achieve competitive advantage, while leaving others to provide non-core services.

1.14 Prahalad and Hamel identified three characteristics of core competencies.

- They are activities that add value in the eyes of the customer.
- They are scarce and difficult for competitors to imitate.
- They are flexible in light of the organisation's future needs.

Suppliers as part of a supply chain

1.15 Of course, once an organisation has accepted that it must buy some (at least) of its supplies from external sources, it accepts also that it must engage in some kind of relationship with external suppliers. We have already seen that in modern thinking this implies a need to manage not just internal activities, but all activities along the organisation's supply chain.

1.16 We have looked at aspects of supply chain management in earlier chapters and will return to it in the final chapter of this Course Book. In the meantime, you should just bear in mind that a need to buy supplies externally implies a need to manage an upstream supply chain.

2 The outsourcing decision

Make/do or buy?

2.1 Make/do or buy decisions face all organisations. Where the activity concerned is one that the organisation could conceivably do itself we refer also to an 'outsourcing' decision – ie we decide whether to do the activity in-house or whether to source from an outside supplier. (We would not use the term 'outsourcing' in the context of a decision to buy, say, utility supplies from a utilities company, because this is not something that most organisations could feasibly undertake in-house.)

2.2 From the product concept stage organisations can look to make everything (ie only buy raw materials) or to outsource everything (ie buy everything from external suppliers). The decision is based on a number of factors.

- Strategic planning
- Production capacity (whether this refers to manufacturing capability, or the ability to perform service activities by means of suitably qualified internal staff)
- Suitable external suppliers
- Relationships with suppliers
- Effects on the internal workforce
- Labour market conditions
- Sales forecasts

2.3 Modern business practice favours specialist outsource providers and subcontractors where appropriate. The modern focus on core competencies has led many companies to buy in products, components or assemblies previously produced in-house, and to outsource a range of support functions (such as maintenance, catering, warehousing and transport, and staff recruitment and training) and even core functions such as sales and customer service (eg in call centres).

2.4 Well managed links with suppliers are established to enable the development of 'supply chain' thinking through all tiers of the supply chain to reduce areas of waste and cost and to improve areas such as quality.

2.5 Make/do or buy decisions depend on a range of strategic and operational factors. Outsourcing distances organisations from their market and the long-term effects must be fully considered.

- The effects on total costs of production
- Profitability, risk and flexibility
- The availability of in-house competencies and capacity; how readily they can be acquired or expanded; and whether they will be consistently available in future. (Lack of adequate competency or capacity will push the firm towards the 'buy' end of the spectrum.)
- The availability of suitable external suppliers. A lack of suitable suppliers would push the firm towards the 'make/do' end of the spectrum.
- The need to retain knowledge and skill in-house for future applications.
- Human resource impacts. Will a decision to buy from outside lead to redundancies? Will a decision to make/do in-house lead to a need for training and/or recruitment?

2.6 Outsourcing is the strategic use of resources to perform activities traditionally handled by internal staff and their resources. It is a management strategy where an organisation devolves responsibility for operating non-core functions to specialised service providers.

2.7 Lysons and Farrington in *Purchasing and Supply Chain Management* explain the difference between outsourcing and subcontracting in that outsourcing is a long-term strategic decision while subcontracting is a tactical short-term approach.

2.8 Broadly speaking, the advantages and disadvantages of strategic outsourcing can be summarised as in Table 6.1.

Table 6.1 *Advantages and disadvantages of strategic outsourcing*

ADVANTAGES	DISADVANTAGES
Support for downsizing: reduction in staffing, space and facilities costs	Costs of services and relationship or contract management
Allows focused investment of managerial, staff and other resources on core or distinctive competencies	Loss of control and difficulties ensuring service standards
Leverages the specialist expertise, technologies, resources and economies of scale of suppliers, with potential to add more value at less cost than the organisation could achieve itself (for non-core activities)	Potential reputational damage if service or ethical issues arise
Enables synergy through collaborative supply relationships	Loss of in-house knowledge and competencies (for future needs)
	Loss of control over confidential information and intellectual property
	Ethical and employee relations issues of downsizing

What activities should be outsourced?

2.9 Strategic outsourcing should only be applied to non-core competencies, activities for which external contractors have required competence and capability, or activities for which value for money is offered by outsourcing in relation to the service levels that can be obtained. This may arise from the supplier's cost and profit structure, economies of scale, or potential for the buyer to dispose of assets.

2.10 Non-core competencies can be outsourced in cases where the outsourced services:

- Will benefit from the expertise, cost efficiency and synergy of specialist suppliers
- Will enable the firm to leverage its core competencies (ie to get maximum advantage from them)
- Will not disadvantage the organisation with loss of in-house capability or vulnerability to market risks
- Will enable the firm to exploit technology or other operational capabilities which it lacks (and would find too costly to develop) in-house.

2.11 In relation to the competency of external contractors, various options are summarised in a simple matrix devised by Ray Carter: Figure 6.1. The matrix suggests that the ideal candidates for outsourcing are activities which are of low core importance and for which there are external suppliers who are highly competent.

Figure 6.1 *A matrix for the outsourcing decision*

		Competence of contractors High	*Competence of contractors* Low
Core importance	Low	**Outsource/buy in**	**Develop contracting**
Core importance	High	**Collaboration**	**In-house**

2.12 Organisations must be fully aware of the optimum capacity level of their operations. The need is to maximise the use of our manufacturing facilities in order to gain economies of scale in production and maximum profitability.

2.13 To operate at the optimum capacity level requires planning and foresight from operations management. Make-or-buy decisions are fundamental to any business, either manufacturing or service. Do we make in-house? Do we invest in machinery and/or technology? Do we staff the operation? Do we provide for the overhead costs of the operation? Do we need to control the operation internally as core to our business? Have we the skills to manufacture in-house? Or do we buy in from outside?

Outsourcing and value for money

2.14 Clearly a major reason for outsourcing is the possibility that it will be cheaper to buy the services than to provide them in-house. This is not necessarily an easy matter to establish, and assessing value for money in outsourced services is a delicate process.

2.15 The first step is to learn as much as the supplier is willing to disclose of his cost and profit structure. This will facilitate comparison with alternatives.

2.16 The overall cost of the service would obviously be compared with prices offered by alternative suppliers, and possibly with the costs of in-house operation if these are known. (They may not be if it is a new type of service that is being bought.)

2.17 More crucially, the effectiveness of the supplier must be evaluated by a comparison of actual outputs achieved with the original objectives specified. This of course implies that the buying organisation starts with a clear idea of what it needs and what it expects to get. The involvement of purchasing professionals in the early stages can be of great assistance.

2.18 It may not be completely obvious why a third party should be able to carry out the same service more cheaply than can be achieved in-house. However, it is possible that the supplier benefits from economies of scale in the particular activity we are outsourcing. Or they may benefit from greater productivity and efficiency arising from the volume of transactions they handle and the specialist experience they possess.

2.19 Apart from actual cost savings, the organisation can achieve a leaner balance sheet by disposing of assets that would otherwise be required in-house. This can have a favourable impact on the financial stability of the company.

Costs involved in outsourcing

2.20 The buyer must also reckon on significant costs attached to the exercise. These are summarised in Table 6.2.

Table 6.2 *The costs involved in outsourcing*

COST	EXPLANATION
Preliminary costs	The costs of preparing and analysing the business case, the costs of identifying potential suppliers, the costs of the supplier selection process, the costs of agreeing terms and drawing up the contract
Contractual price	The actual sums payable to the supplier under the terms of the contract – hopefully, these will represent a reduction compared with current expenditure
Costs of getting it wrong	Costs arising if the supplier fails to perform
Costs of getting it right	Cost of all activities designed to ensure successful completion of the contract – changes to systems and processes, transitional difficulties, contract management costs, communication costs etc
Hidden costs	Costs of buying staff helping to implement the contract, costs of vagueness or ambiguity in the specification (leading to unexpected difficulties), costs of over-specifying etc.

Operational reasons for outsourcing

2.21 Costs are always an important issue, but there are other reasons why organisations may wish to outsource. For example, the outsourcer may be unable to keep up with the pace of technological change in a particular activity. Attempting to do so would divert management attention from the more important tasks of running the business effectively. This is a reason why many companies have outsourced their IT applications.

2.22 Another reason may be that we are simply not very good at the activity in question. Rather than attempting to improve our performance in an area that is not core to our business, it may be preferable to use the expert services of an organisation specialising in that activity.

Why does it go wrong?

2.23 Numerous surveys, together with anecdotal evidence, suggest that outsourcing projects often fail to deliver the expected benefits. Some of the possible reasons for this are listed below.

- The organisation fails to distinguish correctly between core and non-core activities.
- The organisation fails to identify and select a suitable supplier, leading to poor performance of the outsourced activity, or in the worst cases to supplier failure.
- The outsourcing contract contains inadequate or inappropriate terms and conditions.
- The contract does not contain well defined key performance indicators or service levels, which means that it is difficult to establish where things are going wrong.
- The organisation gradually surrenders control of performance to the contractor.

2.24 Much of this can be avoided if the outsourcing exercise is carefully planned within a defined strategic framework.

3 Outsourcing in practice

Core and non-core activities

3.1 Organisations have been understandably reluctant to outsource activities that they regard as core, ie activities that embody their key competencies and that confer competitive advantage. Any other activities have been regarded as possible candidates for outsourcing. Clearly the decision to outsource an activity can only be taken after a strategic assessment of what activities are core and non-core.

3.2 Once the candidates for outsourcing have been identified, the organisation must consider various criteria by which the decision can be evaluated. These will include both value for money and operational factors.

3.3 Outsourcing is the ultimate expression of a buyer's attitude to a supplier as an extension of in-house resources. Facilities or functions that were produced in-house are instead performed by external contractors working very closely with the buying organisation.

3.4 In many cases the same personnel carry out the outsourced tasks, only instead of being employed by the buyer they work for the contractor. There are instances where the original staff remain *in situ*, and even work on the same equipment; the only difference is in the status of the staff (they now work for the contractor, not for the buyer) and the ownership of the equipment (transferred from buyer to contractor).

The terminology of outsourcing

3.5 Table 6.3 sets out some important definitions and explanations of terminology that you should be familiar with.

Table 6.3 *Terminology relating to outsourcing*

DEFINITION	EXPLANATION
A service contract is a supply contract concerned with provision of a service rather than a tangible product.	This is the simplest case. The buyer wishes to purchase a service, eg a consultancy assignment, and enters into a contract with a selected supplier.
Subcontracting is the use of an outside organisation to do work that we cannot do ourselves because of a temporary shortage of resources.	Company A contracts Company B (the main contractor) to perform certain work. Company B could do all the work itself, but has too much work on at present. To meet Company A's deadline, B subcontracts some of the work to C.
Outsourcing is the delegation of work previously carried out in-house to an external service provider.	The outsourcer will draw up a contract, typically for the long term, specifying the work to be done, the service levels to be achieved etc. The outsourcer retains responsibility for satisfactory completion of the work, but delegates day-to-day operations to the outsource provider.
Insourcing is the opposite of outsourcing.	The organisation previously outsourced the work, but now decides to bring it in-house.

3.6 Outsourcing has been used in respect of many different functions. Organisations have contracted with external suppliers to provide cleaning or catering services previously performed by internal staff; banks have outsourced their information systems development to specialist external consultancies; major international businesses have outsourced their accounting and tax planning functions to firms of chartered accountants; and so on.

3.7 Gary J Zenz has a useful analysis of the steps that managers should take to make a success of outsourcing.

- Managers should establish a strategy for the proper balancing of management, contracting and consulting.
- Managers should establish a strategy to deal with possible reductions in staff.
- Managers should closely integrate the external suppliers.
- Managers should provide appropriate communication channels.

3.8 Zenz also identifies the questionable assumptions that sometimes underlie the decision to outsource. 'The problem with outsourcing is that while a series of incremental outsourcing decisions, taken individually, make economic sense, collectively they represent the surrender of the business's competitive advantage.'

The impact on supplier relations

3.9 Outsourcing has some implications for commercial relationships with external suppliers.

- The organisation now has a dependence on an external supplier where none existed before.
- The organisation needs to consider what type of relationship it should be developing with the supplier.
- Many individuals within the organisation might be slow to recognise the implications of the change, and continue to treat the outsourced service as something that 'belongs' to the organisation. This can lead to difficulties in the relationship.
- The newly-established supplier organisation might fail to recognise the importance of delivering a high-value service, and could take an opportunistic approach, offering an unsatisfactory service or charging an excessive price.

- To be long-lasting, there should be a 'performance-driven' partnership, where the customer and supplier develop a partnership rather than have a cosy relationship, and the supplier recognises the need to seek excellence in performance
- There is no reason why the organisation should continue to use the new supplier for its outsourced services. There is a possibility of putting the outsourced service to competitive tendering from a number of potential suppliers.

Identifying suitable performance measures

3.10 To ensure that the supplier is performing to the required standard, it is important to identify suitable performance measures. Often these will be specified in the contract.

3.11 Needless to say, the measures chosen will depend very much on the details of the particular agreement. But in all cases they will include measures relating to cost and measures relating to service quality. Some measures will be 'hard', in the sense that they can be assessed objectively (eg the time taken to deal with a complaint or difficulty); others will be 'soft', in the sense that they are to some extent subjective. For example, the buyer will be concerned with the politeness of the supplier's staff, but this is not something that can easily be measured.

3.12 To define suitable performance measures, the buyer must focus on the key objectives of the outsource contract. Clearly, the measures chosen must be related to these so that they provide a good indication of how well the relationship is working. It is also important to keep the measurement process simple: a small number of easily understood indicators is preferable to a proliferation of complicated measures.

3.13 Communication is also important. The supplier must be aware of the measures regarded as important by the buyer. This is an important guideline for him in planning his work so as to satisfy the contractual requirements. He must accept that the measures are reasonable in the light of the contract. And communication is of course a two-way process: if the supplier is already performing similar services for other clients he may be able to suggest suitable performance measures from previous experience.

Insourcing

6

3.14 **Insourcing** is the opposite of outsourcing, and involves an organisation taking work in-house, having previously outsourced it.

3.15 An obvious reason why organisations might do this is that the outsource provider might not be doing a very good job. There may be problems with service quality, or the supplier may not be delivering the expected cost savings. In this case it will be appropriate to terminate the contract.

3.16 Even here, though, one might expect the organisation to find an alternative provider. Presumably the work will be insourced only if the organisation believes that no external organisation is able to perform satisfactorily and at an economic price. However, there are other possibilities. For example, the organisation may have re-thought its conclusions on what activities are core and non-core. If it now believes that the activity is core, it may take it in-house for general strategic reasons.

3.17 Although there is nothing inherent in the term 'outsourcing' to refer to the purchase of services, it is normally used in the service context. The problems of buying services have become increasingly important for purchasing professionals as the general expenditure on services throughout the economy has risen. We have seen in the previous chapter that the purchase of services presents buyers with problems additional to those that arise in purchasing manufactured goods. We re-cap these below.

- Manufactured goods are tangible: they can be inspected and tested before purchase. Services are intangible.
- Goods emerging from a manufacturing process almost certainly have a high degree of uniformity which simplifies their evaluation. Every separate instance of service provision is unique and may or may not be equivalent to previous instances.
- The exact purpose for which a manufactured good is used will usually be known and its suitability can therefore be assessed objectively. It is harder to assess the many factors comprised in provision of a service: for example, what weight should be placed on the friendliness or smart appearance of the supplier's staff, compared with their basic efficiency in doing the job?
- A manufactured good is usually purchased for immediate use in some well defined way, such as incorporation in a larger product or onward sale. A service may be purchased for a long period, during which requirements may change subtly from the original specification.
- When purchasing a manufactured good a buyer can usually identify a number of suppliers offering products with essentially similar features (including price). Services are different: the offering from one supplier will inevitably differ from those of other suppliers in a whole range of mostly intangible ways.

Service level agreements

3.18 A crucial element in the success of external service provision is to reach clear agreement on the level of service to be provided.

3.19 The buyer needs to investigate the supplier's plans with some care. For example, he should enquire about the rates that the supplier intends to pay his staff. If these appear to be below average there is a potential impact on the quality of service likely to be delivered. This is particularly the case when the service is high on labour content.

3.20 Where services are currently being provided by in-house staff it is important to determine whether existing service levels are adequate. If they are not, it is not sufficient to require a similar level of service from the new supplier. Instead, defined improvements to the current level of service must be agreed in advance.

Quality assurance in services

3.21 By far the most important measure for assuring quality in service provision is the initial specification. Without detailed agreement on what is required it is most unlikely that the purchaser will be satisfied with what is eventually provided. However, even after the most thorough advance preparation it is not safe to assume that responsibility can simply be handed over entirely to the service provider. On the contrary, the purchasing organisation must closely monitor the delivery of the service.

3.22 The role of the user department is vital. They are best able to determine whether their needs are being met, and if not whether this arises from fault of the supplier or inadequate specification.

3.23 An important aid to assuring quality is the establishment of collaborative relationships. The supplier must be made to feel some 'ownership' in the service being provided, and to sense some loyalty between his own organisation and that of his customer.

3.24 Before entering into this kind of collaborative relationship it is up to the buyer to pursue traditional purchasing disciplines in his selection of the supplier. For example, he must be sure that the supplier is not of the type to fall into a common temptation in these situations: that of 'buying' the business by means of a low quote, with the intention of raising prices sharply once the buyer has become dependent.

3.25 The financial security of the supplier is also important. Remember that if a purchaser abandons internal provision of a service it is hard to re-establish it. To find at this stage that your supplier is in danger of insolvency is very bad news indeed.

3.26 A feature of this kind of agreement is that requirements change over time. Sometimes this results from external pressures; for example, new legislation on health and safety might mean that certain activities are more costly than expected. In other cases the needs of the user department simply evolve over time. In either case, buyers must be aware both of the cost implications and of the need to ensure that service provision is adjusted in the way required.

3.27 Note the concept of service quality gaps, ie the differences in perception that may arise between supplier and buyer. Four categories of 'gap' are identified.

- Consumer expectations, ie the gap between what consumers actually expect and what managers perceive that they expect
- Managers' perceptions of consumers' expectations, ie the gap between what consumers actually want and what managers lay down in service quality specifications
- Service quality specifications – the gap between what is delivered and what is specified
- Actual service delivery, ie the external communications gap between provider and customer.

Outsourcing the logistics function

3.28 An important strand in modern management thinking is the need to concentrate on core activities in order to secure competitive advantage. The consequence of this philosophy is that more use is made of external suppliers for activities previously provided in-house. In the remainder of this chapter we give examples of some functions that are often outsourced, beginning with the logistics function.

3.29 Most manufacturers regard logistics as a support function rather than as a core activity. Even those who still maintain an 'own-account' logistics operation are willing to make use of contractors to a greater or lesser extent.

3.30 The potential benefits that may be realised by manufacturers include the following.

- Contracting out frees up resources – above all, financial capital and management time – which can more profitably be devoted to core activities.
- Logistics specialists are well placed to recognise and respond to rising customer expectations. This would be a serious management burden if distribution remained in-house.
- Contracting out gives greater flexibility in times of difficulty. Firms with their own operation may suffer if employees go on strike, or if demand is very variable during the year. Access to outside specialists enables these risks to be spread.

- Buying firms gain access to specialist expertise which may enable them to develop improved distribution systems, offering better service than customers would otherwise have received.

3.31 All of these benefits presuppose that the external contracting is conducted on the basis of long-term relationships with a small number of suppliers. For example, any saving in management time would quickly be dissipated if negotiations with new suppliers, and the process of familiarisation, were ongoing; ideally, this should be a one-off exercise.

3.32 Despite the benefits outlined above, not all manufacturers are willing to outsource the logistics function. Several reasons may be suggested for this.

- Most fundamentally, a firm may be concerned that outside contractors will not give the required level of service. There has been some justification for such a view in the historical development of specialist logistics suppliers. Nowadays, however, the range of services offered has increased, standards are high, and advances in information technology have enabled buying firms to monitor the service provided very closely.
- A firm may fear that a large number of separate outside contractors – for storage, materials handling, haulage etc – would complicate matters. This too has been a justified worry in the past, but can now be overcome by making use of one of the various contractors that offer an integrated service covering all logistics areas.
- Finally, reluctance may stem from a general policy of wishing to retain control. Handing over major functional areas lock, stock and barrel to external suppliers runs counter to this natural instinct. Again, the solution lies within the varied offerings available from logistics providers. These range from management-only contracts (in which the buyer retains ownership of logistics assets, but contracts out their management), through various forms of joint venture, to full system takeover by the outside specialist.

Outsourcing information systems

3.33 An area where outsourcing has become particularly prevalent in recent years is that of information systems (IS). Many organisations have handed over their data processing functions, and in some cases their systems development functions as well, to external specialists.

3.34 The technical complexity of this area makes it an attractive candidate for outsourcing. The cost of maintaining IS expertise in house is high. But in some cases the move to outsourcing has been made for the wrong reasons. Some organisations have despaired of being able to solve particular problems in their IT systems and have looked to outsource providers for solutions.

3.35 Outsourcing consultants are unanimous in condemning this approach. As with all outsourcing, the objective should be to draw on specialist expertise, not to abandon all responsibility for the outsourced activity. A consultant quoted in *Supply Management* summed it up as follows: 'The management that wants to outsource problems in order to get rid of them is a disaster waiting to happen. You've got to solve the problems first before you outsource'.

3.36 Even assuming that management are outsourcing for the right reasons, it remains difficult to measure the success of the project. The main problem is in defining the level of service. It is highly unlikely that one outsourcing supplier will offer exactly the same level of service as another, which means that the costs they quote are not strictly comparable. At the level of detail, what one supplier is offering to do will differ from the other's offering.

3.37 In practice this will lead to serious problems of evaluation, but once again it is clear that a proactive purchasing function has an important role to play. Essentially, the problem is one of specification: the buyer must know in advance, and in detail, exactly what he requires the supplier to provide. In the light of a detailed specification it will be much easier to monitor performance and to assess value for money.

Outsourcing facilities management

3.38 We have looked above at some specific services that may be outsourced, such as logistics services or IT services. A more radical approach to this general issue goes by the name of facilities management. Under this kind of agreement a specialist facilities management company is contracted to run services such as buildings maintenance, catering, heating and lighting, security and waste disposal.

3.39 At its extreme this approach is summed up in the words of a car manufacturer wishing to open an overseas manufacturing facility. 'Provide everything I need in support services: that's what I pay you for. All I want to do is make cars.' In a case like this the facilities management company will take on a very wide range of responsibilities, and the manufacturer must be certain that service provision will be up to the appropriate standard and at the right cost.

3.40 Experts in the field believe that the impulse towards outsourcing comes not from cost considerations (though of course value for money is important), but from a wish for greater efficiency. Buyers want to tap in to specialist expertise so as to increase the quality of service.

3.41 Another stimulus to this kind of agreement has undoubtedly been a desire to share risks. Buyers have sometimes welcomed the idea that if things go wrong it is an outside contractor that is to blame. While this may be regarded as a somewhat negative attitude – it would be better to concentrate on ensuring that things **don't** go wrong – it does highlight the fact that there are indeed serious risks in the services underpinning a company's operations.

3.42 Some of these risks were amusingly summarised in a 'nightmare' facilities management contract devised by a firm of solicitors specialising in the field. In their fictional example a company suffered the following series of disasters.

- Staff walked out after failing to receive their wages because of a technical problem with the payroll.
- Other staff left when the heating failed on an unexpectedly cold Autumn day.
- A subcontractor wiped out all the information on a customer database.
- Staff suffered food poisoning because of hygiene failures in the canteen.

3.43 The scale of these problems underlines the importance of quality assurance in all cases where services are outsourced.

Shared services

3.44 So far we have looked at the outsourcing of services to an external supplier. However, an alternative is to set up an internal department to provide services such as finance, human resources, information technology etc: **shared service units**.

3.45 Reasons for keeping shared services in-house include the following.

- Costs may be cheaper if we do not pay a profit margin to an outside supplier.
- There may be no suitable provider externally.

- There may be reasons of confidentiality.
- By keeping the activity in-house we retain control over quality.

3.46 Despite these reasons, organisations increasingly look to outsource non-core functions. This is in line with the arguments of Prahalad and Hamel (see earlier in this chapter), but also reflects certain disadvantages of using internally provided services.

- Absence of competition can lead to complacency within the internal department providing the service.
- Similarly, there may be a lack of efficiency, innovation and customer responsiveness.
- There are no economies of scale, as the internal provider has only one customer.

3.47 These drawbacks must be weighed against the advantages of internal supply.

- The transaction costs are low, because there is no process of supplier identification, supplier evaluation, tendering etc to go through.
- The relationship between 'customer' and 'supplier' is likely to be long-term and stable, enabling the supplier to hone the service in line with customer requirements.
- There is (usually) no profit motive within the internal supplier, which means that they can concentrate instead on the quality of service offered.
- Customer and supplier are part of the same organisation, meaning that they should share the same culture and values.

Chapter summary

- An organisation of even modest size needs a wide range of supplies in order to carry out its activities. It is inconceivable that all such supplies can be produced internally; hence the need for purchases from external suppliers.
- In practice, most organisations will concentrate on internal production of the things they are good at. Other necessary supplies they will source from outside.
- The make/do or buy decision is a strategic one, based on an analysis of the organisation's particular competencies.
- A matrix developed by Ray Carter suggests that the best candidates for outsourcing are activities where the core importance (to the focal firm) is slight, and there are competent contractors to provide the supply.
- A decision to outsource has important implications for relationships with suppliers.
- It is very important to develop suitable measures for evaluating the performance of an outsource provider.

Self-test questions

Numbers in brackets refer to the paragraphs where you can check your answers.

1 Explain what is meant by the make/do or buy decision. (1.4)

2 Distinguish between threshold competencies and core competencies. (1.10, 1.11)

3 List three characteristics of core competencies, as identified by Prahalad and Hamel. (1.14)

4 List factors possibly involved in the make/do or buy decision. (2.2)

5 List possible advantages and disadvantages of strategic outsourcing. (Table 6.1)

6 Sketch Carter's outsourcing matrix. (Figure 6.1)

7 What categories of cost may be incurred as part of an outsourcing decision? (Table 6.2)

8 Distinguish between outsourcing and subcontracting. (2.7 and Table 6.3)

9 Why might an organisation cease outsourcing an activity and take it back in house? (3.15, 3.16)

10 How can a buying organisation assure quality in provision of an outsourced service? (3.21ff)

CHAPTER 7

The Sourcing Process

Assessment criteria and indicative content

3.1 Describe the main stages of a sourcing process

- Identification of needs
- Producing specifications
- Requesting quotations
- Receiving quotations
- Assessing suppliers' quotations
- Making contract award recommendations
- Contract authorisation
- Order placement, blanket orders/frameworks and call off orders
- Performance and delivery
- Payment of suppliers
- Expediting deliveries
- Reviewing outcomes and processes
- Pre and post award stages of a sourcing process

Section headings

1 Requisitions and specifications
2 The sourcing phase
3 Competitive bidding or tendering
4 Contract award
5 Performance, delivery and payment
6 Reviewing outcomes and processes
7 Pre-award and post-award stages

1 Requisitions and specifications

Introduction

1.1 Purchasing procedures and policies will naturally vary widely from one organisation to another – and even within organisations, according to different types of purchases. However, there are certain stages which a 'typical' purchasing transaction will involve, and this is known as the 'purchasing cycle'.

1.2 It may seem a bit odd to have placed coverage of this 'overview' topic so late in the syllabus: many aspects have already been touched on in connection with earlier topics. Broadly, we are moving in this chapter from 'principles' (eg the five rights) to 'procedures': putting the principles into practice.

1.3 In this chapter, we will look at the various stages of the purchasing cycle, and at what happens during each stage. Our descriptions accord with general best practice – but of course we cannot incorporate all of the variations that will be experienced in your professional work. You will need to follow the policies and procedures of your own organisation in your day-to-day work – and will need to pay careful attention to the context of any case study presented by CIPS in your assessment.

Identification of needs

1.4 Before any purchasing transaction can begin, someone must notice that something is needed which is not currently available, and this need must be notified to the purchasing department.

1.5 The need may be identified by a user department: for example, a designer may recognise the need for new software. Or the driver for purchase may come from a stores department: a check of inventory levels may reveal the need to replenish stocks of materials or components.

1.6 In either case, the normal procedure would be for the department concerned to issue a purchase requisition. This form describes the item needed and instigates action by the purchasing department. Typically, the originator of the requisition would keep a copy of the form, while the other copy is forwarded as appropriate.

- If the originator is the stores department, the copy is forwarded to the purchasing department.
- If the originator is a user department, the copy is forwarded to stores. Stores will meet the need if the item is in stock, and if not will pass the requisition on to purchasing.

1.7 A purchase requisition form (whether printed or electronic) will typically include the following details.

- A description of the product or service required: identified by brand name or model number (if known), or accompanied by the specification (if already available)
- The quantity required
- The delivery or provision date
- The internal department code, or budgetary code, to which the expenditure is to be charged
- The name and signature of the originator of the requisition, and its date. This may act as an official authorisation of the need, giving purchasing authority to act upon it, so the signature should be that of an individual with appropriate authority.

1.8 If the organisation operates a materials requirements planning (MRP) system, the identification of the need may instead be signalled by a **bill of materials (BOM)**. Briefly, the approach is to forecast the manufacturing schedule for finished products, and to translate this into details of the materials and parts needed for production: the bill of materials. This can then be compared with stock files, where relevant, to establish which materials and parts are already in stock, and which items will have to be purchased.

Producing specifications

1.9 Whether a requisition or a bill of materials is used, the form will contain details of the required item(s) in a standardised form. It would be wrong to assume that purchasing simply act on this description without enquiry. On the contrary, purchasing must check the requirement carefully, drawing on their past experience of the item and on records of past purchases.

1.10 In many cases it will be appropriate to refer the requisition back to the originator. This may simply be for clarification if the requisition is unclear, but may also be to suggest alternatives that offer better quality or lower price than the item specified. Purchasing should not make such changes without consultation because they cannot know all the factors that the originator may have had in mind when drawing up the requisition. But neither should they accept requisitions without question.

1.11 The process so far relates to the identification and description of the need *within* the buying organisation. The next step will be to establish and/or to communicate a detailed description of the requirement to potential suppliers. Detailed descriptions may already exist (if the purchase is a re-buy), but for new products or services, they may have to be drawn up, in the form of:

- Specifications (of various types)
- Service level agreements (added to the specification of services)
- Contract terms which set out the obligations of buyer and seller in relation to the fulfilment of the specification.

1.12 It is worth mentioning at this point that this is not solely the responsibility of the buyer. The user of the item must also play a part in ensuring that the supplier is providing what is needed to satisfy the requirement.

1.13 For further detail about the production of specifications you should refer back to Chapter 4.

2 The sourcing phase

Identifying and appraising potential suppliers

2.1 Buyers need to carry out a search for potential suppliers and make a list of potential suppliers. Sometimes this part of the process can be omitted if a product is only available from a single, known source. However, buyers should remember that circumstances change and should take steps to ensure that they are not missing new opportunities.

2.2 The list should be reduced by eliminating suppliers who are unable to meet the requirements. Once unsuitable suppliers have been eliminated, the best supplier(s) can be selected. It may be that no single supplier can meet the need in full so more than one may need to be selected.

2.3 It is common for a buyer to contact a number of suppliers in search of quotations.. The general principle is that the successful supplier will be the one with the lowest price. However, there is more to it than this. A supply need may be defined by means of a performance or functional specification, and there may need to be discussion and analysis to decide whether and how effectively each quotation meets the requirements. Even amongst suppliers that do meet the basic requirement, there may be considerable variety in the product and total solution 'package' being offered.

2.4 Buyers need to negotiate with the selected supplier to agree terms. The object of these negotiations should not be for one side to win at the expense of the other side but to come to an arrangement which meets the needs of both. When the negotiations have been completed successfully, the purchase can proceed. The amount of negotiation needed is likely to reflect the complexity of the requirement.

2.5 If it is a routine purchase from a known supplier a purchase order containing the company's standard terms and conditions may be sufficient. In legal terms this would be the basis of a contract, provided the supplier accepts it. However, buyers need to be careful that the supplier does not put his conflicting terms and conditions on the paperwork because this will override the buyer's terms.

Different types of purchase

2.6 There may well be a large list of potential suppliers. Buyers will be aware of them partly from past experience and partly from the department's records. The task at this stage is to narrow down the possibilities.

2.7 Where the item required is a standard or routine one, these stages of the sourcing cycle may be by-passed: preferred or approved suppliers will already be identified, and perhaps contracted on a standing basis. For example, we may already have agreed **framework agreements** or **call-off contracts**, whereby the buyer contracts to source requirements – as and when needed – from the supplier, and purchasers and users can simply 'call off' orders on the agreed terms, as needs arise.

2.8 However, if a new or non-standard item is needed, it will be important to locate, investigate and appraise potential suppliers. The extent of this investigation must be proportionate to the importance and value of the item. It would not be worth the time and cost of detailed supplier appraisal for a purchase of light bulbs, say. It will be essential, however, for strategic or non-standard items; for major high-value purchases (eg capital equipment); for potential long-term partnership relations with a supplier; and for international sourcing and outsourcing (because of the risks involved).

2.9 In the case of major purchases buyers will need to conduct extensive investigations, perhaps involving discussions with salesmen and visits to suppliers' premises. Eventually the list will be narrowed down to a small number of suppliers who, in the buyer's opinion, are well qualified to supply the item(s) required.

2.10 At this point it will be necessary to establish price and availability of the required item(s). The easiest situation is where a low-volume standard item is in question. It is usually possible in such cases to simply refer to suppliers' catalogues and price lists.

2.11 In more complicated cases – for example where large sums of money are at stake, or the item is a non-standard one to be manufactured specially – this approach is insufficient. The buyer must then choose either to negotiate with a small number of suppliers over price and availability, or to request quotations.

Surveying and sourcing the market

2.12 'Surveying the market' means identifying or locating suppliers that may potentially be able to supply the requirement. Buyers will constantly be monitoring the supply market(s) relevant to their organisation's requirements, as well as the performance of the existing supplier base. They may also carry out formal supply market research for a given requirement.

2.13 Sources of information about potential suppliers may include: internal records (with existing, past and potential supplier details and performance appraisals); supplier catalogues, sales force presentations and websites; printed and online directories of suppliers and stockists; price comparison websites; online market exchanges or auction sites (such as e-Bay in the consumer sector); trade or industry exhibitions and conferences; and networking with other buyers (who may be willing to give recommendations and referrals to suppliers with whom they have been satisfied).

2.14 From these preliminary investigations, there may well be a large list of potential suppliers. 'Sourcing the market' involves narrowing down the possibilities and accessing or making contact with shortlisted potential suppliers.

2.15 Suppliers may be shortlisted according to a variety of criteria: size or production capacity, price, reputation, recommendation – and perhaps the buyer's sustainability policies (eg buyers may wish to use small or local suppliers where possible). Potentially interesting suppliers may be contacted by telephone or email to request a brochure or catalogue, a visit to the buyer by the supplier's sales representative, or a visit by the buyer to the supplier.

Appraising suppliers

2.16 In order to avoid wasting time and resources (for both buyer and supplier), shortlisted potential suppliers should generally be *pre-qualified* before they are invited to quote or tender for a contract. Requests for quotation will only be sent to suppliers which the buyer already *knows* to be capable of fulfilling the requirement. This requires the appraisal, evaluation or auditing of potential suppliers.

2.17 A range of criteria may be used to appraise potential suppliers. One model frequently referred to in the purchasing literature, for example, is **Carter's 10 Cs**.

- *Competence* of the supplier to fulfil the contract
- *Capacity* of the supplier to meet the purchaser's current and future needs
- *Commitment* of the supplier to quality, service and cost management
- *Control* systems in place for monitoring and managing resources and risks
- *Cash* resources for financial stability
- *Consistency* in delivering and improving levels of quality and service
- *Cost* and value for money
- *Cultural compatibility* of the supplier with the buyer
- *Clean and compliant* performance, in terms of environmental and CSR objectives
- *Communication* efficiency and technology.

2.18 This information may be acquired by various means: appraisal questionnaires completed by suppliers (although the buyer will need to verify the truth and accuracy of information provided by the supplier); perusal of the supplier's financial statements and reports; checking the supplier's certifications, accreditations, quality awards, policy statements and so on; arranging to get references from existing customers; and checking product samples or portfolios of work.

2.19 Once a shortlist of potential suppliers has been identified, the buyer may use a **supplier audit**, **site visit** or **capability survey**: visits to the supplier's premises by a cross-functional appraisal team (eg with experts on purchasing, quality and engineering, say) which shares responsibility for the decision to approve or reject the supplier on the basis of their observations.

2.20 Following the appraisal process, one or more suppliers may be officially recognised as being able to meet the standards and requirements of the particular buyer, and therefore eligible for invitations to quote or tender for contracts: this is known as **supplier approval**. The approval may be for a one-off tender, or may mean that the supplier is put on a list of approved suppliers from which user-department purchasers can source products as required.

Requesting quotations

2.21 The requirement can be signalled to pre-qualified or approved suppliers in various ways, depending on the type of purchase and company policy.

2.22 The organisation may have different procedures in place for orders of different volume or value. For order values under $100, say, there may be no formal requirement for supplier selection. For orders between $100 and $5,000, there may be a negotiation process, or three suppliers may be requested to provide quotations, to ensure competitive pricing. For orders over $5,000 in value, a full competitive bidding or tendering process may be required.

2.23 The organisation may already have negotiated a **framework agreement** or standing contract with a supplier, to meet a requirement of a certain type. In such a case, the requirement will simply be notified by purchase or **call-off order**, on the pre-agreed terms.

2.24 There may be only one available supplier, or the organisation may have negotiated a preferred supplier or sole supplier agreement with a dependable supply partner. In such a case, the buyer may simply negotiate a contract with the preferred or designated supplier.

2.25 In other cases, the organisation may send an 'enquiry' to one or more shortlisted suppliers, also called a **request for quotation** (RFQ). The RFQ will set out the details of the requirement.

- Quantity and description of items required
- Required delivery date and address for delivery
- Special requirements relating to packaging and/or materials handling (eg must be supplied on pallets)
- Terms and conditions of purchase, usually the buyer's standard terms
- Terms of payment
- Contact details: contact name, address, telephone number, email details, reference number to use in reply, date by which to reply

2.26 It will then invite the supplier(s) to submit a proposal and price for the job. These may be evaluated in various ways.

- On a competitive basis: eg the best value bid or quotation 'wins' the contract (as in competitive bidding or tendering)
- As a basis for negotiation with a preferred supplier. (Note, however, that it is not ethical practice to solicit quotations from more than one supplier if you have already decided where the contract will be awarded – eg just to 'motivate' a preferred supplier.)

2.27 In the normal case the various suppliers contacted will reply by quoting their best price for supplying what the buyer wants. However, there is a more exceptional case, namely the possible existence of a supplier **cartel**. This refers to collusion between suppliers, whereby they agree among themselves not to compete on price.

2.28 Such an agreement, being anti-competitive in nature, is illegal. However, buyers need to be aware of the possibility of illegal collusion. Here are some possible signs of this.

- All the prices offered by suppliers are higher than expected.
- One or more suppliers are reluctant to negotiate.
- One or more suppliers have declined to quote.
- The lowest price offered is significantly lower than all the rest. The suggestion here is that all of the other prices have been pitched artificially high.

2.29 Leaving aside this exceptional case, suppliers will usually respond to the enquiry by supplying a quotation. Usually the supplier's quotation will be regarded as constituting an offer which the buyer may or may not wish to accept.

Receiving quotations

2.30 Once the suppliers' quotations have been received, the buyer will need to analyse them to see which one provides the best value to his organisation. If the buyer's requirement is very simple, there will be little difference between the various quotations except in price. Subject to reasonable undertakings on delivery and quality, the buyer will most likely choose the supplier offering the lowest price.

2.31 However, not all transactions are this simple. For example, suppose the buyer is aiming to buy 20 laptop computers for use by senior managers in the organisation.

- There will be differences in the specifications of the machines offered by different suppliers. Presumably all the offerings will at least match the minimum requirements laid down by the buyer, but some machines will exceed that specification. How valuable, if at all, are the additional features?
- There will be differences in the level of support offered by the suppliers (for example, some may offer a one-year warranty at an additional cost, while others may include a three-year warranty in the basic quoted price). How valuable, if at all, is the extra support?
- There may be differences between the buyer's standard terms and conditions and those quoted by the supplier. How amenable is the supplier likely to be in negotiating terms, and how important are the differences anyway?

2.32 This discussion is meant to illustrate that, in the case of even a moderately complex buying requirement, there will be a range of factors (other than basic price) for the buyer to consider in evaluating the supplier quotations. Here are some examples.

- Previous performance of the supplier (including financial stability, reliability etc)
- Delivery lead time
- Add-on costs (freight, insurance, installation and training etc)
- Running costs (including energy efficiency)
- Warranty terms
- Availability of spares
- Availability of maintenance cover
- Ability to upgrade to higher specification
- Risk of obsolescence
- Payment terms
- Residual value and disposal costs
- In the case of overseas suppliers, exchange rates, taxes and import duties

Negotiation

2.33 Negotiation may be the main approach by which contract terms are arrived at, or may be used in evaluating quotations (eg to improve aspects of the preferred quotation, or to ensure that all aspects of the requirement, bid and contract are understood).

2.34 Negotiation is a massive area of study in its own right, but basically, in the purchasing context, it is: 'A process of planning, reviewing and analysing used by a buyer and a seller to reach acceptable agreements or compromises [which] include all aspects of the business transaction, not just price'. [Dobler *et al*]

2.35 The process is summed up by Gennard and Judge as one of:

- *Purposeful persuasion*: each party tries to persuade the other to accept its case or see its viewpoint and
- *Constructive compromise*: both parties accept the need to move closer to each other's position, identifying the areas of common ground where there is room for concessions to be made.

2.36 Negotiation is often broken down into distinct stages or steps – and there are many different ways in which this can be done, as a glance at standard purchasing texts will confirm. A representative sample is shown in Table 7.1.

Table 7.1 *Models of negotiation*

KENNEDY	GREENHALGH	BAILY ET AL
Prepare: what do we want?	Preparation	Pre-negotiation phase
Debate: what do they want?	Relationship building	Negotiation/interaction phase
Propose: what wants might we trade?	Information gathering	Post-negotiation follow-up
Bargain: what wants will we trade?	Information using	
	Bidding	
	Closing the deal	
	Implementing the agreement	

2.37 Objectives should be ranked as high priority, medium priority or low priority. Most negotiations depend on concessions from both sides, and this ranking procedure will help negotiators to determine where they can best afford to give ground or make concessions (low priority objectives) and which areas are non-negotiable (high priority objectives). If one side's low priority (easy to concede) objectives coincide with the other's medium or high priority (valuable to gain) objectives, there is significant potential for constructive bargaining.

2.38 The intricacies of bargaining strategy and technique are well beyond the scope of this syllabus, but it is helpful for both parties to determine two parameters in respect of each objective: the best position that they can reasonably hope for, and the worst position that they are prepared to accept. Where the two acceptable ranges overlap there is scope for negotiation. This is illustrated in Figure 7.1.

Figure 7.1 *Defining the range of negotiation*

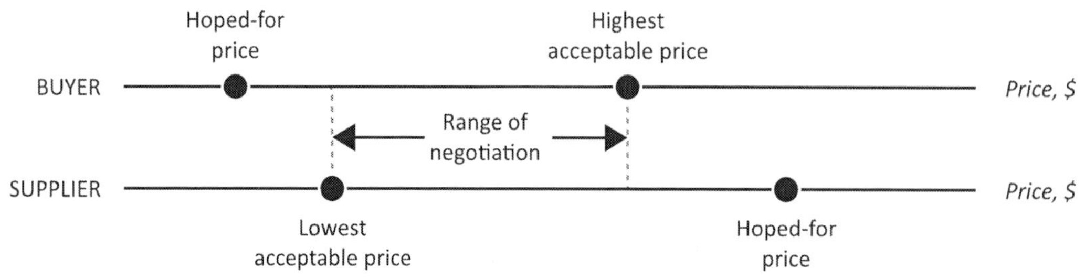

2.39 A range of skills and attributes is required for successful negotiation, including: verbal and non-verbal communication skills; the ability to manage emotions (particularly in conflict situations); assertive communication (non-aggressive, clear, open, confident); flexibility (to respond to changing tactics and opportunities); a range of influencing skills and techniques (eg rational persuasion, emotional appeal); and the ability to formulate proposals and counter-proposals, and to calculate concessions and gains, as the negotiation progresses.

3 Competitive bidding or tendering

The mechanics of tendering

3.1 For particularly complex supply needs a more formal system of quotations may be used. This is known as competitive bidding or tendering. (Indeed, as we will see below, even relatively simple supply needs may be subject to this procedure if the buyer is a public sector organisation.)

3.2 In a tendering procedure, pre-qualified suppliers are issued with an invitation to tender (ITT), or an invitation to bid for a contract, with the buyer intending to choose the one submitting the best proposal or the lowest price.

3.3 Tendering is the process by which suppliers are invited to put themselves forward (or 'bid') for a contract. There are two basic approaches to this.

- **Selective tendering**, in which potential suppliers are pre-qualified and 3–10 suppliers are shortlisted for invitation to tender – as discussed above
- **Open tendering**, in which the invitation to tender is widely advertised and open to any potential bidder.

3.4 When should a buyer use competitive bidding rather than a negotiation? Dobler and Burt (*Purchasing & Supply Management*) give the following guidelines for making the decision: Table 7.2.

Table 7.2 *The use of competitive bidding*

FIVE CRITERIA FOR THE USE OF COMPETITIVE BIDDING	FOUR SITUATIONS IN WHICH COMPETITIVE BIDDING SHOULD NOT BE USED
The value of the purchase should be high enough to justify the expense of the process	It is impossible to estimate production costs accurately
The specifications must be clear and the potential suppliers must have a clear idea of the costs involved in fulfilling the contract	Price is not the only or most important criterion in the award of the contract
There must be an adequate number of potential suppliers in the market	Changes to specification are likely as the contract progresses
The potential suppliers must be both technically qualified and keen for the business	Special tooling or set-up costs are major factors
There must be sufficient time for the procedure to be carried out	

3.5 There are several advantages to competitive bidding or tendering. It ensures fairness and genuine competition between suppliers. It ensures that purchasing decisions are soundly based on cost and value for money. It also secures a wide choice of suppliers, particularly if open tendering is used.

3.6 However, there are also drawbacks, particularly to open tendering processes.

- Wide competition may discourage potentially suitable bidders.
- There may be inadequate pre-qualification of bidders, creating the risk of capability or capacity problems emerging late in the process.
- Competition based primarily on the lowest price may put insufficient focus on important criteria such as quality and sustainability: the lowest-price bid may not represent the best long-term value.
- Tendering also places a potentially large administrative burden on buyers.
- Contract award may be a one-off, not leading suppliers to expect further business. In other words, tenders do not result in deepening buyer-supplier relationships. This may lead to a widening of the supplier base (whereas the modern trend is to favour closer relationships with fewer suppliers). There may also be little incentive for suppliers to perform to the highest standard (as a committed, loyal supply chain partner might do), over and above compliance with the minimum standards set by the specification.

Competitive bidding in the public sector

3.7 For buyers in public sector organisations, open competitive tendering is *compulsory* for contracts above a certain (low) value threshold. This requirement is laid down in EU procurement directives in order to stimulate fair and open competition. Many non-EU countries have similar regulations. However, where the buyer has a choice, selective tendering will usually be used, because it:

- Is less time-consuming and costly for both buyer and suppliers
- Does not present late problems with technical capability or capacity
- Is less frustrating for non-pre-qualified suppliers who may incur the trouble and expense of tendering without having a realistic chance of succeeding.

3.8 The purposes of public sector procurement regulations are broadly as follows.

- To open up the choice of potential suppliers for public sector organisations and utilities, in order to stimulate competition and reduce costs
- To open up new, non-discriminatory and competitive markets for suppliers
- To ensure the free movement of goods and services within the European Union
- To ensure that public sector purchasing decisions are based on value for money (via competition) and that public sector bodies award contracts efficiently and without discrimination.

Assessing suppliers' quotations

3.9 It is important for any invitation to tender to state clearly that the buyer will not be bound to accept the lowest price quoted, and that post-tender negotiation may be entered into if necessary to qualify or clarify tenders, or to discuss potential improvements or adjustments to suppliers' offers.

3.10 Table 7.3 summarises the main points to take account of in evaluating tenders.

Table 7.3 *A checklist for analysing tenders*

1.	Establish a routine for receiving and opening tenders, distributing copies as appropriate and ensuring security.
2.	Set out clearly the responsibilities of the departments involved.
3.	Establish objective award criteria. These should have been set out in the initial invitation to tender, particularly if the contract is subject to statutory control.
4.	Establish teams for the appraisal of each tender, ensuring that the required team members will be available during the time they are required.
5.	Establish a standardised format for logging and reporting on tenders.
6.	Check that the tenders received comply with the award criteria. Non-price criteria (eg technical and production capability, financial stability, CSR and environmental policies, or quality assurance accreditation) will need to be carefully reviewed (and more details sought if required), if suppliers have not been pre-qualified.
7.	Check the arithmetical accuracy of each tender.
8.	Eliminate suppliers whose total quoted price is above the lowest quotes by a specified percentage. (For example, eliminate any supplier whose quoted price is more than 20% above the average of the lowest two quotes.)
9.	Evaluate the tenders in accordance with predetermined checklists for technical, contractual and financial details.
10.	Prepare a report on each tender for submission to the project manager (and as a basis for feedback to unsuccessful bidders, where relevant).

4 Contract award

A spectrum of possibilities

4.1 There is a continuum of relationships that a buyer may have with a supplier, ranging from an arm's length 'transactional' relationship, to a closer 'partnership' relationship at the other extreme. In practice, it is rare to achieve full partnership relations and usually there will be much less commitment on both sides.

4.2 In ascending order of commitment we might identify the following possible relationships.

- Spot buying. This means that a buyer contacts a supplier as a one-off transaction as and when required. See below for more detail on spot buying.
- Regular trading. Very common in practice, this describes the situation where a buyer looking for a particular item on a regular basis usually chooses a particular supplier to satisfy the need.
- Blanket ordering (sometimes called a **call-off contract**). The buyer sets up an agreement on terms and conditions (a **framework agreement**) in relation to a particular item or items. As and when necessary, the buyer 'calls off' his requirements and asks the supplier to deliver in accordance with the framework agreement. A variation on this is known as **system contracting**. Again, see below for further detail.
- Fixed contract. This is one step on from blanket ordering. The additional element is that the fixed contract specifies the total quantities that will eventually be called off.
- Partnership sourcing. Buyer and supplier work together to achieve mutual benefits. For example, the supplier may be involved in early design stages of a new product.

4.3 What factors might influence the choice of relationship in particular cases? Here are a few of the possibilities.

7

- Importance of the item being purchased. If the buyer is dealing with a critical item he is more inclined to favour a close relationship with the supplier.
- Capabilities of suppliers. Close relationships usually involve shared approaches to total quality management and other 'world class' techniques. Some suppliers will simply not be able to cope with this.
- General conditions in the supply market. If there are many competing suppliers, all involved in markets requiring constant innovation, a buyer may be reluctant to commit to a long-term deal with any one of them, because he may be 'backing the wrong horse'.
- Geographical location. It is more difficult to maintain close relationships with a supplier who is geographically distant, though of course modern communications technology is gradually changing this.

Spot buying

4.4 Spot buying is a natural and simple method of purchasing. The buyer sees a need, and simply contacts a supplier to fulfil the need – end of story. There is little administrative effort needed and transaction costs are low. Buyer and supplier simply need to agree on price.

4.5 Spot buying may be used for purchases fulfilling the following criteria.

- The goods are easily specified.
- The goods are needed immediately.
- The order can be fulfilled at once, and payment can be made at once.
- Agreed terms of trade exist.

4.6 Of course, there are dangers. Where prices fluctuate over time, there is a risk of buying at an unfavourable moment. This is particularly the case with volatile commodities such as agricultural crops.

Blanket ordering

4.7 One of the simplest and most common of the variations is **blanket ordering**. This is an agreement under which a supplier undertakes to provide an estimated quantity of items over an agreed period of time at an agreed price. Sometimes the price is not specified in monetary amount, and instead the agreement contains a formula for determining it. For example, the agreement may specify 'market price' and include a method of defining the market price at any time.

4.8 When the buyer needs a delivery of the items he initiates a simplified 'release' procedure which avoids the need to go through all the stages of the traditional purchasing cycle. In simple cases, the buyer simply telephones the supplier and calls for a particular quantity, specifying the blanket order under which the supply has been agreed. Indeed, once the basic agreement has been established it may not be necessary for purchasing staff to become involved in calling for releases. This can be left to user departments instead, though they would be acting under authority delegated by purchasing.

4.9 The quantity of items to be supplied is not usually agreed in advance. Instead, the agreement specifies that the purchaser is to supply all the buyer's requirements for that particular item over an agreed period. In this case, the buyer will provide the supplier with an estimate of requirements in advance, but actual quantities will not be finally known until the end of the agreement.

4.10 The great advantage of this type of agreement arises in the case of items with low unit value, but for which there is a large requirement. The exact number required may be difficult to calculate, and the exact timing of requirements may be even trickier, but the approximate pattern over a period of, say, one year is well enough known for the supplier to be able to plan production and respond when required.

4.11 A typical application for this technique is in the ordering of **consumable office supplies** such as computer stationery. The advantages are that it cuts out the staff time and paperwork that would be involved in numerous small orders, and assures regular supply.

4.12 Buyers must work hard to ensure that blanket orders are handled in a way that makes them satisfactory to suppliers. Otherwise, it will be difficult to obtain agreement. A common problem in this context is unrealistic (inflated) estimates of annual requirements. However, if handled properly blanket orders carry benefits to suppliers as well, particularly in the elimination of selling costs once the order is in effect and in the assurance of a good sales volume for a defined period ahead.

Systems contracts

4.13 A systems contract is a closer form of cooperation between buyer and supplier than a blanket order. Like a blanket order, a systems contract is designed to minimise administrative time and cost in dealing with materials that are subject to constant and repetitive demand. Unlike blanket orders, a **systems contract** (as the term is usually understood) does not relate to a single item or small group of items, but instead covers a large group of materials or supplies. Typically, it is for a long (even indefinite) period.

4.14 The procedure involves negotiation of a master contract specifying the items included in the agreement, the price of each and the terms of delivery. Quantities are not usually specified. When demand arises, appropriate staff (normally from user departments rather than purchasing) call for releases against the contract. Requisitions and purchase orders are not used, so cutting down administration.

4.15 The use of systems contracting implies a high degree of trust on the part of both buyer and supplier. Invariably, the buyer is placing the contract on an exclusive basis (ie no other supplier is to be used when demand arises for one of the specified products). The supplier is faced with uncertain demand and a high requirement for service performance. It is usual to treat the supplier in effect as an extension of the buyer's stores function, and expected delivery times are similar to what would be expected if that were indeed the case. Both buyer and supplier must be prepared for a level of interdependence.

4.16 To make the concept work, there must be a catalogue of the products covered by the agreement. This will contain price details, which is one reason why paperwork is minimised: accounts staff do not need copies of purchase orders in order to check prices, and indeed there is usually no need for a purchase order at all. The supplier receives payment on a periodic basis, say monthly, for all requisitions supplied during the period.

4.17 If the agreement works well, there are significant benefits to the purchaser.

- Administration is reduced.
- Delivery times are rapid.

- Stocks are reduced. This is the effect of having the supplier act like an extension of the stores function, and for this reason systems contracting is sometimes referred to as **stockless purchasing**. It is usually a condition of the contract that the supplier holds a certain level of stock to meet urgent orders from the buyer.
- Purchasing staff are freed up to perform more useful work on high-value items and to play a more strategic role in the organisation.

4.18 The supplier benefits too from the reduction in paperwork and administrative effort. As with blanket ordering, there is also a saving in sales effort for the supplier.

Placing the order

4.19 For simple purchases, which do not require a negotiated contract, the buyer may make out a *purchase order*. In most cases this will be a standard form produced within the organisation. The effect of the form will be to create legal obligations, and for this reason firms are careful to design their purchase orders very carefully, including the legal terms on which they propose to do business.

4.20 In some cases an order may be placed by telephone. This may be because some kind of blanket order system is in place. If this is not the case, then any telephone order should be confirmed later in writing.

4.21 A number of copies of the purchase order are prepared so that appropriate departments can be informed. Obviously the top copy goes to the supplier. Often the supplier receives a second copy too, so that he can sign and return it as evidence that he accepts the order and the legal terms contained on it. One copy will be retained by the purchasing department. Other copies may be sent to the stores department, finance department, and user department, depending on the system within each organisation.

Contract documentation

4.22 Typically, the components for the actual contract will be the specification and/or invitation to tender, the supplier's written proposal, plus any terms or modifications which may have been agreed in negotiation. The contract should be issued in duplicate and signed by both parties, with each party retaining an original copy.

4.23 Where practical, all contract papers should be bound together in date order, and a duplicate copy issued for the supplier's retention, so that both parties can be satisfied as to the completeness of contract documentation. Any subsequent contract variations should be attached to all the copies as and when they are issued.

The post-award phase

4.24 Once a purchase is under way, a new 'sub-cycle' of activity is required to follow it through to completion. This is often called the **purchase-to-pay** or **P2P cycle**, and can be depicted as a two-way flow of transactions as seen in Figure 7.2.

Figure 7.2 *Purchase-to-pay activities*

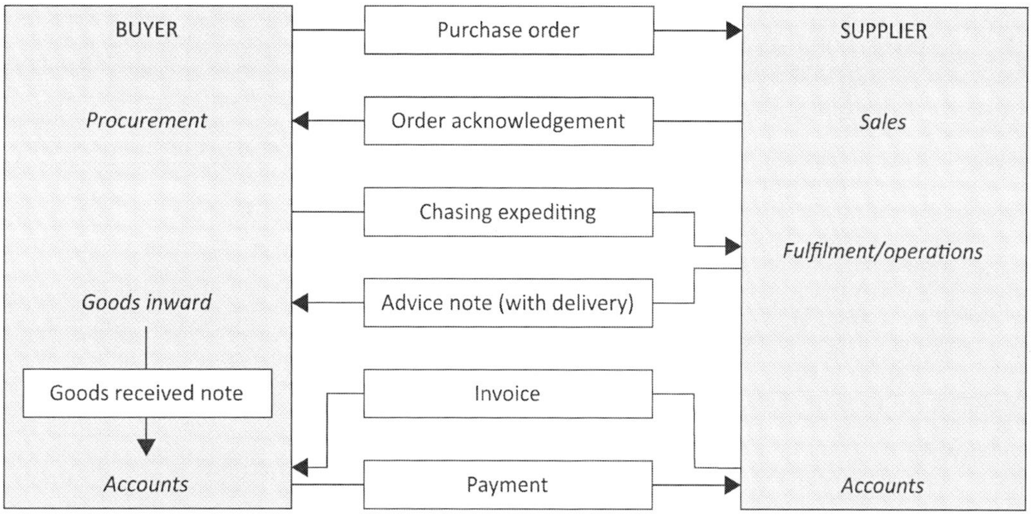

5 Performance, delivery and payment

Delivering the goods

5.1 When an order of goods is ready for delivery, a number of routines usually follow in a defined procedure.

- The supplier sends an advice *note* to the buyer with (or in advance of) delivery of the goods, to notify the buyer of the content and time of the delivery.
- The Goods Inwards department of the buying organisation receives and inspects the goods (by referring to the contract or purchase order), to check that the supplier has delivered the correct goods in the correct quantity, without obvious quality defects. The goods must correspond to what was ordered.
- The goods will normally arrive accompanied by two documents: a consignment note which says how many boxes the delivery consists of; and a delivery note which says what the boxes contain. If the correct number of boxes has been received, delivery can be accepted but it should be specified that it was 'received uninspected'. This allows the delivery vehicle to leave without waiting for the contents of the boxes to be checked
- The Goods Inwards department sends a *goods received note* (GRN) to the purchasing and accounts departments, to indicate that the goods have arrived. This will also note any discrepancies or defects in the order, which the purchasing department will need to raise and resolve with the supplier, prior to authorisation of payment.

5.2 When checking the contents against the purchase order, things to look out for include:

- The part number of each item. If an item cannot be identified – perhaps because the supplier has changed the part number – the goods need to be isolated until the matter has been taken up with the supplier.
- The condition of the goods. If there are any damaged or poor quality goods, they should be isolated and the supplier should be informed. In certain circumstances it may be necessary to carry out a more formal and rigorous inspection to ensure that the goods conform to the specification.
- The quantity of the goods. There are two documents involved – the purchase order and

the delivery note – and the goods themselves. All three must align if the goods are to be accepted.

5.3 The various possibilities are summarised in Table 7.4.

Table 7.4 *Processing receipt of goods from supplier*

QUANTITY ORDERED	DELIVERY NOTE QUANTITY	PHYSICAL QUANTITY	ACTION TO TAKE
10	10	10	Receipt correct, book goods into stock
10	3	3	Book 3 into stock, check 7 to follow later
10	10	5	Problem – isolate goods and take the matter up with our supplier
10	10	15	Problem – isolate goods and take the matter up with our supplier
10	15	15	Problem – isolate goods and take the matter up with our supplier
10	15	10	Problem – isolate goods and take the matter up with our supplier
10	5	10	Problem – isolate goods and take the matter up with our supplier
10	15	12	Problem – isolate goods and take the matter up with our supplier

Expediting deliveries

5.4 It is not safe to assume that the transaction is complete once the order has been placed. There will often be a need to follow-up, chase or 'expedite' an order. The buyer may chase the supplier to return the acknowledgement copy of the purchase order, for example, or check that the delivery will be on schedule, or 'track' the progress of the order and its delivery (eg using online 'track and trace' systems, in which each step in the fulfilment of an order, and its transport, is logged for monitoring).

5.5 Usually, these routines are triggered by review of outstanding orders. In some organisations this may mean reference to a manual file or folder of such orders. More often nowadays, purchase orders are logged on a computer system which will automatically flag when follow-up routines are needed.

5.6 **Expediting** is regarded as a non-value added activity. Such activities are those which add to costs but not to value. It costs money to check delivery schedules and chase suppliers when they are late, but it does not add to the value of the product offered by the organisation. In other words, the organisation is spending money without gaining any value in return.

5.7 Like other non-value adding activities, expediting is increasingly tackled by automation and by approaches that seek to eliminate the need for follow-up. In an ideal world suppliers would perform exactly as required by the time required and no follow-up would be necessary. Until that happy day dawns, though, we must recognise that expediting is an essential part of purchasing work.

Processing discrepancies and rejections

5.8 There are many cases where the transaction does not flow through exactly as anticipated. For example, the supplier may deliver the wrong goods, or the wrong quantity. Alternatively, there may be a problem with the quality of the goods delivered; this might be detected by the inspection department.

5.9 In all such cases the buyer will need to liaise with the supplier to ensure that the matter is resolved. If this leads to disruption to schedules, or to increased costs of inspection, the buyer will seek financial compensation from the supplier.

Auditing the transaction

5.10 The buyer must ensure that the transaction is completed in a way that gives the organisation value for money. There are several aspects to this.

- The goods delivered by the supplier must correspond to what was ordered. This involves agreeing goods received documentation to the purchase order.
- The goods must be of satisfactory quality. This will often be the responsibility of an inspection department.
- The amount charged by the supplier must correspond to the price agreed. This involves checking the supplier's invoice. If the details on the invoice match the goods that were ordered and the goods that were actually delivered, and if the prices on the invoice are those that were agreed before the order was placed, the buyer can approve the invoice and pass it to accounts for payment.

Closing the transaction

5.11 Outstanding orders must be reviewed periodically with a view to taking follow-up action. This may be particularly tricky if part deliveries are made; for example, for an order of 6,000 components a supplier may make three separate deliveries of 2,000 each. Until the final delivery is made the order remains incomplete.

5.12 Once all goods have been received, and the supplier's invoice has been received and checked as described above, it is time to close the transaction. It is usual to do this by noting on the purchase order the details of goods received documentation showing that the goods ordered have actually been received. Similarly, the order may be annotated to reflect the receipt and vouching of the supplier's invoice.

5.13 Once all this has been done, the order may be filed along with other completed orders.

Maintenance of files and records

5.14 Finally, it is important to ensure that all files and records relating to purchase orders are maintained in good order. This makes it easier to investigate any queries that arise later. It also gives buyers a permanent record of how a particular order was satisfied. This can be a vital aid in future purchasing decisions. For example, if the records show that Supplier X performed badly in supplying Component Z then buyers will not make the mistake of using that supplier again.

5.15 The use of computers has greatly simplified this process of record keeping. In addition, once data has been entered onto a computerised system it is easy to generate reports. For example, it would be a simple matter for a computer to summarise all transactions with a particular supplier, or all transactions relating to a particular part or material. This is a great help to buyers in planning future purchases.

Payment of suppliers

5.16 The supplier will in due course send an invoice or request for payment to the buyer. Purchasing should check that it corresponds to the order or contract (in regard to the agreed price) and to the GRN (in regard to goods actually received), and then *either* query discrepancies with the supplier or authorise the invoice for payment and pass it to the accounts department for payment.

5.17 Invoices should be paid within the period stated in the agreed terms of trade: often 30, 60 or 90 days. Credit periods are an issue for cashflow, for both the buyer and the supplier. The buyer may want to pay as late as possible, in order to retain his cash (or earn interest on his banked funds), but the supplier will want to be paid as early as possible, to obtain those same benefits – especially since he has already incurred the cost of supplying the product or service.

5.18 It is part of ethical trading to pay supplier invoices *on time, as agreed*. It also impacts on the buyer's standing as an attractive (or unattractive) customer for suppliers, and on the ongoing relationship with suppliers. An unjustly unpaid invoice may result in stoppage of supply until the matter is settled, and/or the threat of legal action by the supplier. Repeated late payment or disputed payment of invoices can significantly damage the buyer's credibility, the supplier's loyalty and commitment (and therefore future reliability and quality), and in the worst case, the buyer's ability to find suppliers willing to do business.

5.19 Commercial payments are often made by *electronic credit transfer*, through the banking system, which is safe and swift. (One disadvantage, however, is that payments tend to be handled on regular days of the month, on a payment cycle, which may represent a late payment for a supplier, or prevent the buyer from receiving an early payment discount.)

5.20 Another possibility is payment by *corporate credit card* or *purchasing card*, which allows the delegation of routine purchases to user-department staff, and is efficient in terms of invoicing and other transaction costs. However, this may also allow 'maverick' spending by non-purchasing specialists, unless safeguards are in place: eg spending limits on the use of cards, authorised supplier lists and so on.

6 Reviewing outcomes and processes

Introduction

6.1 It is usually beneficial to carry out a review of the entire sourcing process and the outcomes. The results should be recorded so that mistakes can be learned from and any necessary action can be taken. Generally, a review is not as frequently necessary for routine purchases. Buyers should pay attention to the following aspects.

- *Managing performance levels.* Service level agreements (SLAs) and performance measures (such as key performance indicators or KPIs) may be developed to express the desired outputs from the purchase: these documents will form an operational tool with which the respective managers can monitor performance on a day-to-day basis. Such documentation will usually be more flexible than the purchase documentation itself.
- *Contract reviews.* Contract managers from both buyer and supplier organisations should meet periodically to review performance and delivery of contract outputs. There may be regular issues to discuss (eg customer feedback or a complaints log), while other agenda issues will relate to issues arising during the review period.

- *Relationship management:* developing the working relationship between the purchaser and supplier, through regular contacts, communication and information sharing; developing and applying supplier incentives (to motivate suppliers); managing and resolving conflicts; and developing approaches to collaboration and mutual support (including supplier assistance or development).

6.2 Usually, most attention is devoted to deciding whether a supplier has caused issues which need pursuing now, and whether they are worth returning to in the future.

Supplier performance appraisal or vendor rating

6.3 There are various good reasons to put effort into evaluating supplier performance. According to Lysons & Farrington, supplier performance appraisal can:

- Help identify the highest-quality and best-performing suppliers: assisting decision-making regarding: (a) which suppliers should get specific orders (or be invited to tender for a contract); (b) when a supplier should be retained or removed from a preferred or approved list; and (c) which suppliers show potential for closer partnership relationships.
- Suggest how relationships with suppliers can (or need to be) enhanced to improve their performance (eg to evaluate the effectiveness of purchasing's supplier selection and contract management processes)
- Help ensure that suppliers live up to what was promised in their contracts
- Provide suppliers with an incentive to maintain and/or continuously improve performance levels
- Significantly improve supplier performance, by identifying problems which can be tracked and fixed, or areas in which support and development is needed.

6.4 Remember that *supplier appraisal* (pre-contract, for the purposes of supplier selection – see Section 2 of this chapter) is a somewhat different process from *supplier performance appraisal* (post-contract, for the purposes of management control). The former assesses a potential supplier's capability to fulfil the buyer's requirements; the latter assesses a current supplier's performance in fulfilling them. In order to distinguish the two more clearly, the post-contract process is sometimes referred to as **vendor rating**: a vendor being a person or organisation that currently sells you something, and rating being a way of evaluating or 'scoring' performance.

6.5 Vendor rating is the measurement of supplier performance using agreed criteria, usually including:

- *Price*: eg measured by value for money, market price or under, lowest or competitive pricing, good cost management and reasonable profit margins
- *Quality*: eg measured by key performance indicators (KPIs) such as the number or proportion of defects, quality assurance procedures
- *Delivery*: eg measured by KPIs such as the proportion of on-time in-full (OTIF) deliveries, or increases or decreases in lead times for delivery

6.6 Other measurable factors might include: after-sales service, efficiency and accuracy of contract management and administration, willingness to commit to continuous improvement, quality of contacts and communication, contribution to innovation, flexibility and responsiveness to urgent or unusual requests – and so on.

Identifying problems in the purchasing cycle

6.7 We have touched on some of the problems which we can encounter in the purchasing cycle as we have gone along. It's worth emphasising and further explaining them. To make this easier we will divide the problems up by the organisation responsible for them, beginning with the buyer organisation.

- *Unclear specifications*. This is obviously a problem. If our supplier cannot understand our requirements it is virtually impossible for him to meet our requirements. At best an unclear specification may require extra work to put it right. At the worst it could mean the delivery of an unsuitable product. Some areas, particularly services, can be quite difficult to specify. Take, for example, a requirement for office cleaning. Do we have to specify exactly how we want the offices to be cleaned in order to avoid a dispute over what the word 'clean' actually means? What may be entirely satisfactory to our cleaner may be quite unsatisfactory to us.
- *Late ordering*. This can be a considerable problem. At best it might mean that we have to lay on a special delivery with all its consequent costs. At worst it might mean that we run out of stock and can no longer supply our customers' needs. The problem becomes worse as we increase the level of control on our products. It is worth noting that ordering late in a manufacturing environment can bring the whole production line to a halt, involving huge losses.
- *Late booking in*. When stock arrives at our warehouse it should be booked in immediately or, at least, on the same day. If we don't do this we are adding to the lead time of the product and may well over-order the next time around. Also, we may have customers who are waiting to receive the goods.

6.8 There are similar problems which can be generated in the supplier's organisation.

- *Quality*. When the goods arrive at our warehouse, one of the things we must do is check that they are in a suitable condition. If they are not we must arrange for a replacement delivery. However, depending on the proportion of goods that we reject, this problem can range from an irritation to a catastrophe. If, for example, we receive 100 units and reject one this is not quite such a problem as receiving 100 and rejecting 99. In the first instance we have a chance of getting a replacement during the time it takes us to use the remaining 99, whereas in the second instance we have almost no leeway at all.
- *Late delivery*. Just as we said that the late booking of goods into stock can have a bad effect on our customers, so can late delivery. At best this will mean that we use up some of our safety stock but on other occasions we may actually run out completely.
- *Early delivery*. Although not as bad as late delivery, early delivery can cause problems in the warehouse. They may not have the resources to deal with a delivery they were expecting to arrive on Wednesday, if it arrives ahead of time on Monday.

6.9 Although all these problems can occur, the most likely one is late delivery. There are a number of reasons for this, not least the fact that trucks break down, motorways get clogged up and the weather can compound the whole problem. Also, it is quite possible that our supplier does not view our requirement with quite the same urgency as we do. To avoid the worst effects of late delivery we need to have a mechanism in place which allows us to expedite our deliveries.

6.10 A good **expediting system** should prevent problems from arising as well as reacting when a late delivery occurs. However, we should be aware that not every order needs to be expedited and that some products are more important to us as a business than others. An efficient expediting system will, therefore, place our orders into different categories, perhaps like this:

- *'A' type order*. Those thought important enough for us to make a planned visit to the supplier to make sure that nothing is about to go wrong. These products are often referred to as 'strategic' because they are so important to our organisation.
- *'B' type order*. Those that require us to take action by telephone or email. Less important than 'A' orders but, nevertheless, sufficiently important for us to make sure they arrive on time.
- *'C' type order*. Those we need to progress only if our supplier does not deliver the goods by the due date. Although this action is purely reactive we need to know that nothing has gone so wrong that the goods might never arrive.
- *'D' type order*. Those we would progress only if we are specifically asked to. This might occur if a customer decides to order goods from us earlier than expected or we can foresee a need for any other reason.

6.11 We must remember that, if we use a simple system such as that described here, an order may not remain in its allotted category. Some orders may take on a higher priority and others may have a reduced priority.

6.12 Of course we need to make sure that, having categorised our orders, we do in fact expedite them. We can do this with a simple diary or we can set up a computerised system which prompts us by printing a list of orders we need to chase today. It is also important that we should record the results of our expediting to save us doing the same job twice.

Authorisation

6.13 Buyers spend huge sums of money, often a very large proportion of the total earned by the organisations that employ them. It is vital to ensure that the organisation receives full value for the sums spent. To a large extent this is achieved by reliance on the professional expertise of buyers, but that might be insufficient without a defined system of controls.

6.14 In particular, purchasing staff depend on user departments to identify needs. While buyers can use their experience to question requisitions, in the last resort the user department has the most detailed knowledge of their own requirements. This means that care must be taken to avoid inappropriate or irresponsible requisitions.

6.15 This is achieved by authorisation procedures, which take effect at three main points in the purchasing cycle.

- When a requisition is originated it must be signed by an authorised individual before being passed to purchasing. This gives purchasing the assurance they need that the requisition is for an item that is genuinely needed.
- When the purchase order is completed, it must be signed by an authorised person within the purchasing department. The person signing it will usually do so with sight of the requisition and any other relevant documentation.
- When the supplier's invoice is received it is not passed for payment to the accounts department until purchasing staff have carried out the checks already described.

7 Pre-award and post-award stages

The stages of a purchasing cycle

7.1 The purchasing cycle comprises all of the procurement activities that take place from the initial identification of need to the final satisfaction of that need. Virtually every purchasing transaction follows much the same process but the emphasis placed on the different stages varies between transactions. This means that the purchasing cycle is **transferable**: no matter what sector you work in, or what you are trying to buy, you will typically follow the stages in this cycle, or something very similar. The main stages of the purchasing cycle, as identified by the syllabus, are shown in Figure 7.3 (repeated for convenience from Chapter 2).

Figure 7.3 *Generic purchasing cycle shown as three phases*

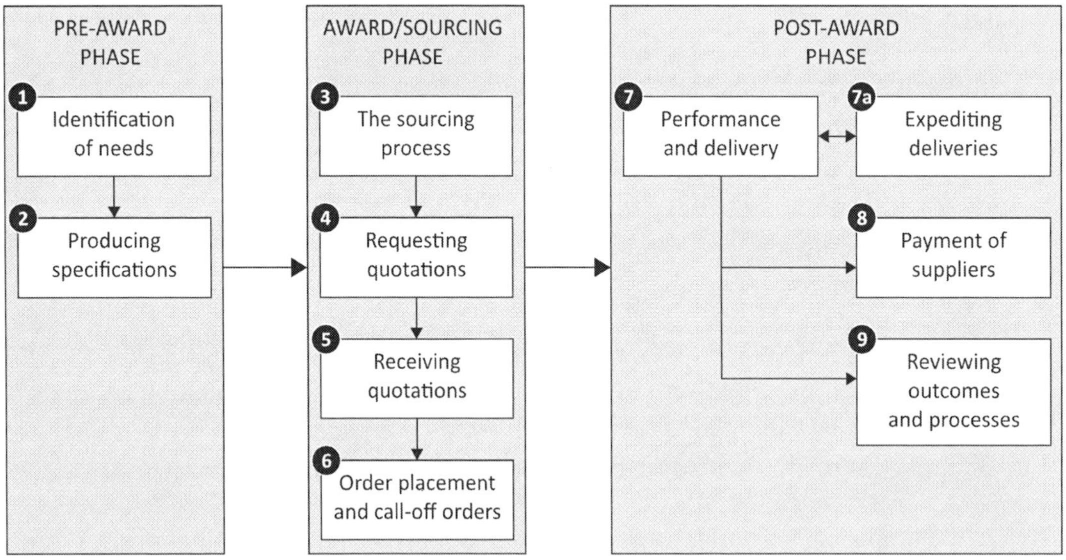

7.2 A note on terminology may be useful here.

- *Sourcing* (pre-award) is the part of the process concerned with 'how and where services or products are obtained' (CIPS): ie requirements definition, tendering, supplier selection and contract award.
- *Purchasing* (post-award) is, more properly, the part of the process concerned with the transactional aspects of purchase: requisitioning, authorising, ordering, receipting and payment. (This is sometimes called the **purchase to pay cycle** or P2P cycle).

7.3 Not every purchase will follow every stage of the cycle. If a purchase is a **straight re-buy** of items already sourced from a supplier, for example, it will not be necessary to establish a specification, survey and source the market, invite quotations and select a supplier: the buyer may already have a preferred supplier (and perhaps a standing purchase agreement or 'call-off contract' with them). If it is a **modified re-buy**, in that some of the requirement has changed, it may be necessary to re-specify the need or re-negotiate the contract, but the same supplier may be used (or *vice versa*: the specification may stay the same, but a new supplier will be sought). **New buys** are more likely to conform to the full cycle.

7.4 However, buyers should always be aware that circumstances can change and should make sure that they are not missing out by ignoring new options.

7.5 The descriptions we give accord with best practice but of course cannot incorporate all of the variation that will be experienced in the course of your professional work in different organisations. Each organisation will lay down policies (outlining the broad objectives to be achieved) and procedures (detailed guidelines for each stage of the process). You will follow the policies and procedures of your own organisation in your day-to-day work, but you should find that they accord closely with the descriptions above.

Some key forms and documents in the purchasing cycle

7.6 You will need to learn to identify, use and explain a range of key forms and documents used in the purchasing cycle. To give you an overview we list them below.

- Purchase requisition or bill of materials (notification by users of a need for purchase)
- Specification and/or service level agreement
- Supplier appraisal questionnaire (for evaluation of potential supplier suitability)
- Request for quotation (RFQ) or invitation to tender (ITT)
- Supplier quotation, bid or tender documents
- Purchase order (or contract)
- Acknowledgement of order (from the supplier)
- Advice note (from the supplier, notifying delivery of the order)
- Goods received note (confirming receipt of the order)
- Quality inspection forms
- Invoice or statement (request for payment)
- Vendor rating forms (for appraising supplier performance).

Chapter summary

- The start of the purchasing cycle is the identification of a need. This is usually signalled by a purchase requisition, or perhaps a bill of materials.
- The next step will often be to communicate the need to a potential supplier, using a specification.
- The extent of the purchasing cycle depends partly on the type of purchase. For some supplies, a framework agreement will already be in place.
- When assessing potential suppliers it is useful to use a formal framework, such as Carter's 10Cs.
- Once quotations are received from suppliers they must be evaluated and compared on an objective basis.
- In some cases – and this is almost always the case in the public sector – a process of tendering is used, either selective or open.
- There is a spectrum of possible buyer-supplier relationships, ranging from spot buying to partnership sourcing.
- When the supplier delivers, it is important to verify the correctness and quality of what has been supplied. Assuming all is in order, payment should be made promptly in accordance with the terms of the supply contract.
- Buyers regularly assess the performance of significant suppliers, sometimes using a formal vendor rating system.

Self-test questions

Numbers in brackets refer to the paragraphs where you can check your answers.

1 What details will a purchase requisition form typically contain? (1.7)

2 Why might a buyer refer a requisition back to the originator? (1.10)

3 What is meant by 'surveying the market'? (2.12)

4 Explain how a framework agreement and call-off order works. (2.23)

5 What factors should a buyer consider when evaluating quotations from suppliers? (2.32)

6 Describe four situations in which tendering should not be used (according to Dobler and Burt). (Table 7.2)

7 What are the purposes of the EU procurement directives? (3.8)

8 Describe 'blanket ordering'. (4.7)

9 What are the benefits of systems contracts to a buyer? (4.17)

10 Why is expediting regarded as a non-value-adding activity? (5.6)

11 What are the reasons for conducting supplier performance appraisal? (6.3)

12 At what stages in the purchasing cycle is a process of authorisation required? (6.15)

CHAPTER 8

Components of a Supply Chain

Assessment criteria and indicative content

4.1 Explain the main components of a supply chain

- Customers and their customers
- Customers and consumers
- Suppliers and their use of suppliers
- Tiers of a supply chain
- The global aspects of supply chains
- Examples of supply chains in action

Section headings

1. Customers, consumers and suppliers
2. Tiers of a supply chain
3. The concept of globalisation
4. Global aspects of supply chains
5. Supply chains in action

1 Customers, consumers and suppliers

The nature of supply chains

1.1 As we saw in Chapter 1, a supply chain is a term covering all activities associated with the flow of goods from the raw materials stage through to the end user. Supply chain management is the art of integrating these activities through improved supply chain relationships in order to obtain sustainable competitive advantage.

1.2 A supply chain may be very short. As an example, you may have driven past a farm and noticed a sign advertising fresh eggs for sale. The farmer is producing the goods and selling direct to his customers with no intermediaries.

1.3 In other cases the supply chain may be very long. For example, if you purchase a washing machine from a department store there will clearly have been many organisations involved in the stages leading up to your purchase. To analyse the supply chain you would have to go right back to the extraction of a metallic ore forming the main material of the washing machine.

1.4 Some supply chains are controlled through ownership. This is the case, for example, with the large oil companies. Typically, these companies have control over all the main stages of exploration, production, refining and retailing. These activities are carried out by organisations within the overall ownership of the oil company.

1.5 In most cases, though, supply chains are controlled through contracts between unrelated parties.

A supplier contracts to provide his customer with required goods or services. The customer may process these supplies before selling them onwards to his own customer, or he may simply on-sell them (in the case of a retailer or wholesaler). These transactions are subject to the contractual terms that prevail between the parties concerned.

1.6 While the concepts of customer and supplier are easily understood, the distinction between customers and consumers may be less clear.

- A customer is the person or organisation that purchases from the supplier.
- The consumer is the person or organisation that uses the final product.

1.7 In some cases, the customer and the consumer may be the same person. For example, if a manufacturer buys a component from a supplier he is both the customer (because he is purchasing from a supplier) and the consumer (because it is the manufacturer that uses the product purchased, for incorporation into his own products).

1.8 But in other cases the distinction may be important. For example, a retailer who purchases a finished product from a wholesaler is a customer (because he has purchased from a supplier), but he is not a consumer (because he does not intend to use the finished product himself – he intends to sell it on to someone else, who becomes the consumer).

A simple supply chain

1.9 The principal flows in a very simple supply chain were shown in Figure 1.2 of Chapter 1 (you should refer back to refresh your memory). We can think of the basic 'stream' as flowing from a first supplier (perhaps a raw material extractor) to a final consumer, so in relation to the firm we are focusing on (the 'focal firm'):

- Suppliers (the firms from which it *buys* the *inputs* to its activities) are said to be **upstream**; and
- Customers (the firms or individuals to whom it *sells* the *outputs* of its activities) are said to be **downstream**.

1.10 If we focus on only two parties (for example, a single supplier and one of its customers, or a single buyer and one of its suppliers), the relationship will be a 'one to one' or 'two-party' (sometimes called 'dyadic') relationship (Figure 8.1).

Figure 8.1 *Dyadic supply relationships*

1.11 However, as we saw in Chapter 1, these kinds of supplier-customer exchanges usually happen within the context of a lengthier supply process: an extractor or producer of raw materials supplies to a processing plant or producer of components, which supplies to a manufacturing or assembly organisation, which supplies to a distributor or retail outlet, which supplies to the consumer. It is this total configuration which is often called a chain, or channel.

Internal and external supply chains

1.12 It is also important to realise that the supply chain concept can be applied *within* commercial organisations – as well as *between* them.

1.13 The **inter-business supply chain** describes the model we have outlined above: a linked sequence of contributors in different firms. Part or all of such a chain may be brought within the control of a single holding company. We have seen that large oil companies, for example, typically have control over all the main stages of exploration, production, refining and retailing. In most cases, however, supply chains are controlled through supply contracts and collaborative relationships between separate, autonomous entities.

1.14 The **internal supply chain** describes a similar flow of information and other resources *within* – into and through – a given organisation: from inbound activities (purchasing and receiving inputs), to conversion activities (transforming inputs into outputs) to outbound activities (moving outputs onward to customers). For example, a road haulage company might have operational units for maintenance and servicing of vehicles, loading and driving. The purchasing department is an internal supplier of tools, machine oil and overalls (among other things) to the mechanics, who are in turn suppliers of repair and maintenance services to the vehicle drivers – who are suppliers of the finished products to the company's external customers.

1.15 Seeing internal processes and relationships as a kind of supply chain therefore highlights the extent to which each function in an organisation acts as a link in the chain which delivers value to end customers. This is an important idea for the **internal customer concept**, which suggests that any unit of a firm whose task contributes to the task of other units can be regarded as a supplier of goods and services to those units. In order to fulfil its objectives, the supplying unit will need to anticipate and satisfy the requirements of these internal customers – just as a supplying firm will seek to do for its external customers.

1.16 The purchasing function is part of the internal supply chain: it is served by internal suppliers (for example, the finance function which provides budgetary reports and finance allocations, and the technical department which provides specifications and requisitions) and in turn serves internal customers (the various other functions on whose behalf it procures supplies, or to whom it gives advice).

Suppliers and their use of suppliers

1.17 It is worth remembering that our picture is simplified. In reality, each organisation in the supply chain has multiple other relationships with its own customers, suppliers, industry contacts, partners and advisers – and even competitors (in trade associations or industry think tanks, say) – any or all of whom may also be connected with each other. Many writers now argue, therefore, that a more appropriate metaphor for the supply process is not a chain, but a network or web. So even the simplest set of relationships might look something like the following: Figure 8.2.

Figure 8.2 *A simple supply network!*

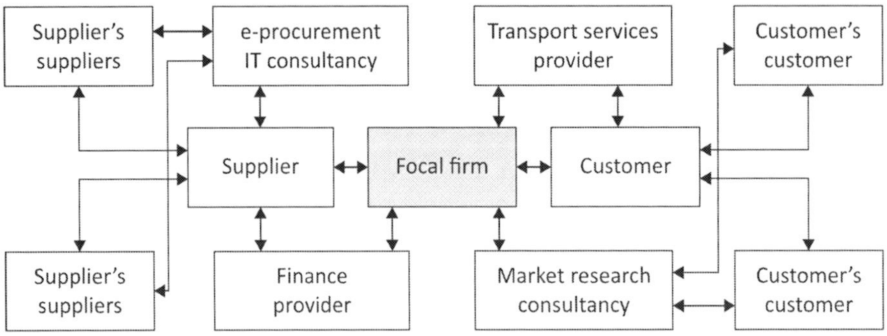

1.18 It is clear from our description of a supply chain, and even clearer from the above depiction of a supply network, that the products or services we supply impact not just on our own direct customers, but on *their* customers (and their customers ...).

1.19 By the same token, a focal firm is dependent on many suppliers with whom it has no direct contact. This emphasises the importance of supply chain management: it is not sufficient to manage our direct suppliers because we are also exposed to *their* suppliers (and their suppliers ...). A buyer's responsibilities must nowadays be seen in the context of an entire supply chain and not just in relation to the firm he works for.

1.20 One approach to dealing with this is known as tiering of a supply chain, which is the subject of the next section.

2 Tiers of a supply chain

2.1 An important strategic issue facing supply organisations is the structure of their supply chains. One such issue is easily illustrated. Suppose that a manufacturer wishes to maximise his own part in the value adding process by taking in only a minimum contribution from outside suppliers. For example, the manufacturer buys in parts from a number of suppliers, and assembles them through a number of stages before the finished product is complete. The structure of the supply chain in such a case is as illustrated in Figure 8.3.

Figure 8.3 *All manufacturing performed by top-level purchaser*

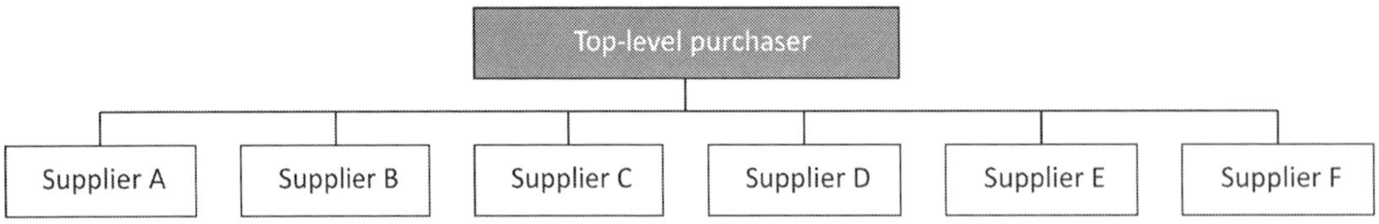

2.2 By contrast, suppose that the manufacturer sees strategic advantage in outsourcing all activities other than the final stages of production. In that case his direct relationship may be (in simplified terms) with a single supplier or (more realistically) with a single tier of suppliers.

2.3 Each supplier in this first tier would have an extensive role to fulfil in the manufacture of the final product. He would discharge this responsibility by making use of 'second tier' suppliers. The structure of the supply chain now looks like Figure 8.4.

Figure 8.4 *Top-level purchaser outsources most manufacturing*

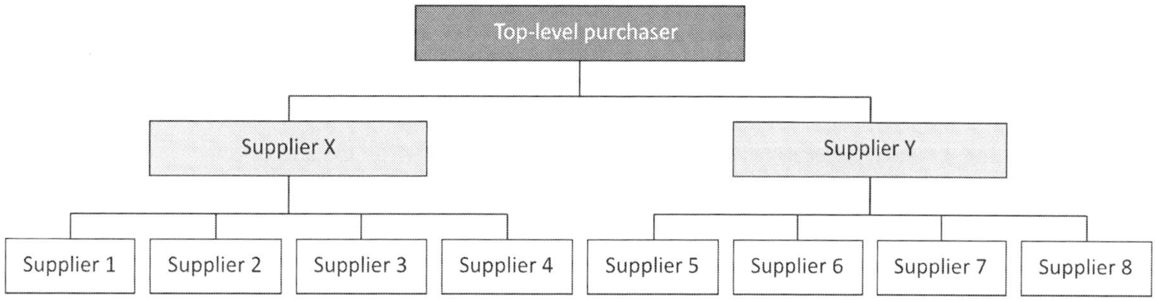

2.4 An organisation might adopt a deliberate policy of tiering its suppliers, so as to reduce the number of first-tier suppliers (suppliers with which it deals directly), and so 'reduce its vendor base'.

2.5 An organisation deals directly only with first-tier suppliers. Second-tier suppliers are suppliers to first-tier suppliers, and deal with the first-tier supplier, not the 'original equipment manufacturer' (OEM).

2.6 For example, an original equipment manufacturer might have 180 different suppliers with which it deals directly. In order to rationalise its commercial relationships, the OEM might pursue a policy of reducing the number of its first-tier suppliers to, say, 20 within a given time frame. To the extent that the OEM still needs products or services from some of the 180 suppliers who are no longer in the first tier, it will be the task of one of the first-tier suppliers to organise the other suppliers, who will become second-tier suppliers.

2.7 In a manufacturing operation, such as automobile manufacture, the OEM is the producer of the end product. First-tier suppliers would tend to be specialist assemblers, each making a particular subassembly. Second-tier suppliers would be component manufacturers, who would supply their products to a first-tier supplier.

2.8 The relationship between an OEM and its first-tier suppliers will be critically important, because each first-tier supplier will be organising the second-tier suppliers for the benefit of the OEM. The OEM will have a limited number of first-tier supplier relationships, and can focus on developing these as a long-term partnership. The first-tier suppliers will be expected to work with the OEM in making improvements and adding value throughout the supply chain, and in developing innovations in products and practices. Improvements in the supply chain will depend heavily on the contributions of the first-tier suppliers.

2.9 The drivers for tiering suppliers might include any of the following.

- The OEM wants to develop long-term relationships with key suppliers, but only has the time and resources to develop a limited number of such relationships.
- Standardisation of parts and variety reduction has reduced the number of parts required, so that the OEM needs fewer suppliers than in the past.
- There has been consolidation of suppliers within the supply market.

2.10 The benefits of tiering may be any or all of the following.

- The OEM has fewer commercial relationships to manage, and can direct its attention to improving these key relationships.

- The OEM can have strategic focus, without having to worry so much about the transactional and operational details of procurement.
- The OEM can share an objective to improve the supply chain with its first-tier suppliers: a shared effort is likely to bring more and better improvements.
- When responsibility is devolved to first-tier suppliers, operational decisions might be taken with a greater understanding of the operational detail, combined with a knowledge of the objectives and requirements of the OEM.
- First-tier suppliers might be able to co-ordinate supply activities more efficiently.

Characteristics of a first-tier supplier

2.11 The characteristics of a typical first-tier supplier are as follows.

- It is a direct supplier to the OEM.
- It is usually a supplier of a high-cost or complex subassembly.
- It is heavily dependent on the OEM, which in turn is heavily dependent on the first-tier supplier. It might even purchase assets dedicated to use on jobs for the OEM.
- There is a close and long-term buyer-supplier relationship with the OEM, and the partnership should ideally operate as a partnership of equals. The OEM should not be a dominant partner.
- It will often be involved in discussing new product ideas with the OEM.
- It is responsible for dealing with a number of second-tier suppliers. This number could be quite large. In effect, the first-tier supplier is put in charge of a section of the OEM's vendor base.
- It understands and shares the 'mission' of the OEM.
- It disseminates the standards and working practices of the OEM to the second-tier suppliers with which it deals.
- It must be a competitive producer to justify selection by the OEM.
- The supplier must also have the management capabilities to manage the second-tier suppliers efficiently.
- The relationship with the OEM is a long-term partnership. For example, the supplier will negotiate ways of removing costs from the supply chain (partnership relationship) rather than negotiate the allocation of costs between the buyer and the supplier.

The effects of tiering: upstream management

2.12 What are the effects of these different structures on management of the supply chain, from the perspective of buyers in the purchasing company at the top of the chain?

2.13 An immediate effect is that such buyers find themselves with far fewer transactions to handle and far fewer suppliers to manage. This greatly simplifies many operational tasks of purchasing.

2.14 At the same time, the purchaser must recognise the extent to which responsibility for his firm's product has been handed over to outsiders. This makes it necessary to ensure that the outsiders are thoroughly up to scratch in all relevant areas. In other words, it suggests that the relationships with suppliers, though fewer in number, will be closer and deeper than under the alternative model.

2.15 In particular, it is likely that the final purchaser will want to drill down through tiers in the supply chain to ensure that appropriate quality is present all the way down. This means that influences on lower-tier suppliers will come not only from the firms immediately above them in the chain, but potentially also from the very top of the chain.

2.16 For first-tier suppliers the implications are also significant. In effect, these suppliers have to take on the main responsibility for investment in product and process development. This implies a need for such suppliers to feel secure of continuing business from the top-level purchaser. Once again, this points to a partnership model of buyer/supplier relationships.

2.17 The competitive environment raises additional issues, particularly in relation to this last point about investment by first-tier suppliers. The top-level purchaser must consider carefully his attitude to these suppliers servicing his competitors as well as his own operations. In some cases, he may feel that this is unacceptable and will make it a condition of awarding the business that first-tier suppliers do not deal with competitors.

2.18 However, this will not always be an option. An important consideration is the level of investment required of the first-tier supplier. If this is very large, the supplier will have to cast his net widely to find other customers and so recoup his outlay. Inevitably, this will mean dealing with firms in the same or similar industries, and this is bound to mean that some customers are competitors of each other.

Controlling the tiered supply base

2.19 The organisation at the head of the tiering arrangement – say, the motor vehicle assembler in the motor industry, such as Ford or Renault – has the power to influence much of what happens lower down among the tiers of suppliers. This is true even in the case of suppliers well down the chain, who have little or no contact with the assembler. The influence spreads down from the top through the tiers.

2.20 As an example of this, a tier-one supplier may be pressured to adopt certain other suppliers at tier two. This may conflict with the tier-one supplier's own preferences. If he is forced to choose a supplier other than his regular partner, the tier-one supplier will feel that his own supply relationships are being damaged. Similarly, there are cases where the top-level purchaser may insist on a particular supplier (of raw materials, say) to be used by all organisations in the supply chain.

2.21 The top-level purchaser will also have a strong influence on costs and prices along the supply chain. In extreme cases, they may be strong enough to insist on price levels that suit themselves, with the threat that suppliers who refuse to play ball will be replaced by others.

2.22 This influence on pricing is strengthened in cases where the top-level purchaser insists on open book costing. By gaining access to suppliers' costing records the OEM can point to cost reductions that are achievable. Suppliers may then be pressured to pass on these benefits to the OEM, rather than benefiting from them directly.

2.23 Finally, the top-level purchaser can influence the systems and processes further down the supply chain. As an example, the OEM may insist on the use of electronic data interchange and barcoding. Suppliers who are not compliant will lose the work. This puts serious pressures on suppliers who are part of more than one supply chain, ultimately supplying more than one OEM: they may have to have more than one suite of systems to meet the respective demands of their top-level purchasers.

Supply chain management (SCM)

2.24 Supply chain management (SCM) is an holistic and strategic approach to supply chain relationships. It may be defined as: 'the *management of relations and integrated business processes across the supply chain* that produces products, services and information that add value for the end customer... Use of the SCM concept entails that the links in the supply chain plan and co-ordinate their processes and relationships by weighing the *overall efficiency and competitive power* of the supply chain'. (*Jespersen & Skjott-Larsen:* italics ours)

2.25 In other words, where supplier management looks mainly at the relationship between the buying firm and its own immediate suppliers, supply chain management looks at the interactions and linkages between all the organisations that make up the supply chain. This is an important distinction.

2.26 SCM consists primarily of building collaborative relationships across the supply chain, so that the whole chain works together to add value for the end customer in a profitable way. *Christopher et al* (2002) argue that, these days:

'The real competitive struggle is not between individual companies, but between their supply chains or networks... What makes a supply chain or network unique is the way the *relationships and interfaces in the chain or network are managed.* In this sense, a major source of differentiation comes from *the quality of relationships that one business enjoys, compared to its competitors.*'

2.27 Andrea Reynolds suggests a number of other pressures in the modern business environment, which act as 'drivers' for SCM.

- Cost pressures (the need to reduce inventory and other wastes)
- Time pressures (the need for faster, more customised deliveries)
- Reliability pressures (the need to ensure that quality and delivery commitments to increasingly demanding customers can be met)
- Response pressures (the need to provide real-time information to increasingly demanding customers)
- Transparency pressures (the need to make the status of orders visible, to support planning)
- Globalisation pressure (the need to co-ordinate multiple, complex global supply networks)

2.28 The benefits of an SCM approach include the following.

- Reduced costs, by eliminating waste activities and implementing cost reduction programmes throughout the supply chain. ('Often there are many activities that do not create value involved in trade between two companies. Jointly locating and eliminating these activities, as well as developing co-operative goals and guidelines for the future, can focus resources on real improvements and development possibilities' *Jespersen & Skjott-Larsen*)
- Improved responsiveness to customers' requirements (by focusing the whole business process on customer satisfaction) – hopefully resulting in greater customer loyalty and sales revenue
- Access to complementary resources and capabilities (eg joint investment in research and development, technology-sharing, ideas-sharing and so on)
- Enhanced product and service quality (eg through collaborative quality management, continuous improvement programmes and improved supplier motivation)
- Improving supply chain communication, which in turn offers benefits for more efficient

planning and co-ordination, reduced inventory, and potential for innovation and flexibility.

- Sharing demand forecasting and planning information enables suppliers to produce only what is required, when it is required – an approach which you may recognise as just in time supply.
- Faster lead times for product development and delivery also mean that new and modified products can be offered in response to changing customer demand – an approach which you may recognise as 'agile' supply.
- Better communication allows greater transparency. Information on costings, performance, and the status of individual orders and stock movements is available quickly or in real time: building trust, and enabling all parties to plan ahead and to manage contingencies as they emerge.

2.29 However, it is important to be realistic about the benefits claimed for SCM – and to analyse whether it is relevant, possible or beneficial for a particular organisation. It is not for everyone! For one thing, it requires considerable investment, internal support and willingness on the part of suppliers and clients – any or all of which may be absent. It also involves focusing on closer relationships with a smaller number of suppliers and clients, and this may be risky (if the relationships don't work out, for example, or if the firm becomes dependent on a supplier which later has problems, or a customer which later 'gets a better offer').

3 The concept of globalisation

3.1 Globalisation may be defined as 'the increasing integration of internationally dispersed economic activity' (Boddy). It is an extension of the supply chain across the national, financial, political, topographical, and cultural divides which previously constrained it.

3.2 This integration may involve the globalisation of *markets.* It has been argued that with worldwide access to media, travel and communications, there has been a convergence of consumer needs and wants: major brands (such as Coca Cola or McDonald's) can be sold worldwide, without much modification for particular geographic markets.

3.3 This opened up new markets and offered economies of scale – but these advantages have proved hard to grasp for some brands, which lost (or failed to gain) market share against locally-adapted brands which catered to specific national and regional cultures, tastes and conditions. (Marks & Spencer, for example, has had a mixed history with its international stores.)

3.4 A parallel development has been the globalisation of *production*. High domestic labour costs, for labour-intensive operations, has enabled intense competition from cheaper imports originating in countries with lower-cost labour. (Think about industries such as electronic goods, clothing, footwear and toy manufacture, for example.)

3.5 This has stimulated the growth of outsourcing, as developed countries have outsourced the production of finished goods and components, and the delivery of service, to countries such as Taiwan, China, South Korea, Singapore, Sri Lanka and India. The media is now full of examples of companies 'offshoring' their administrative work and telephone enquiries (eg major banks) and product assembly (eg Hitachi, Compaq, Mattel).

3.6 The main drivers for any given industry to become globalised (based on Yip, *Total Global Strategy)* include the following: Table 8.1.

Table 8.1 *Drivers for globalisation of an industry*

FACTOR	EXAMPLES
Market factors	• Convergence of customer needs, creating demand for products and services to be available on a worldwide basis • Globalised marketing firms becoming global customers – seeking suppliers who can also operate on a worldwide basis • Transferable marketing, with the development of global communication and distribution channels (including the internet).
Cost factors	• Economies of scale available through the large potential volume of global sales • Sourcing efficiencies, as firms are able to select the lowest-cost supplier from anywhere in the world • Product development costs: where development costs are high, firms will need to extend the earning potential of products by selling into international markets
Government factors	• Trade policies, which have tended to support free markets between nations (reducing protectionist barriers to trade) • Harmonisation of technical standards, which has enabled the sourcing of standardised components, compatible systems etc • Host government policies, aimed at encouraging global operators to base themselves in their countries, eg via tax incentives
Competitive factors	• Companies faced with global competition will have to consider becoming global themselves, in order to stay competitive
Technology factors	• Developments in ICT support and enable: • 'Virtual organisation': sourcing expertise and collaboration regardless of location (eg off-shored administrative centres) • Global supply (eg through access to international supply market information, improved supplier management and monitoring) • Global logistics (eg through computerised transport planning and delivery tracking) • General improvements in international business communication (eg through email)

3.7 It should be obvious from recent events that many people oppose globalisation on the grounds that it is hostile to happy, self-determined life. They put forward the following arguments.

- It encourages the exploitation of labour in developing nations (poor wages, poor conditions, child labour and so on) for lower-cost production.
- It encourages the exploitation of local markets, using them as dumping grounds for poor-quality or obsolete goods, and leading to increased foreign debt.
- It 'exports' pollution, deforestation, urbanisation and other environmental damage to developing nations.
- It undermines governments in the management of their own domestic economies, particularly through the influence of the World Trade Organisation and the power of global corporations (whose turnover exceeds the total economic output of some nations...)
- It causes unemployment in developed nations, where justified expectations of pay and conditions make labour 'uncompetitive' with cheap-labour competitors.
- It squeezes small, local businesses out of markets, with negative effects on competition, communities and cultures. (There is a well-publicised cultural fight-back by small local retailers against giants like WalMart, for example, and by 'slow food' producers against the McDonald's of the world...)
- It encourages the erosion of local cultures and the loss of local languages.

The purchasing perspective

3.8 From the purchasing perspective, increasing globalisation offers opportunities to extend the supply base – the pool of suppliers that a buyer can choose to access. Buyers must nowadays consider, for any particular purchase, whether a local (domestic) supplier or an overseas supplier might be preferable.

3.9 Certain obvious advantages of sourcing locally present themselves immediately. Communications are easier. Delivery costs should be lower. Delivery lead times should be faster and more reliable. Just in time techniques are more likely to be feasible. Rush orders are easier to cope with. No language problems arise. Given all this, why should buyers even consider sourcing from national or international suppliers?

3.10 The most obvious reason is availability of the required materials. There may simply be no local supplier who can meet the requirements. Even if there is, it may well be that a larger national or international supplier benefits from economies of scale that the local firm cannot match, leading to a price and/or quality advantage for the bigger firm.

3.11 Another factor applies in public sector contexts. As we saw in the previous chapter, for countries in the EU (and many countries outside the EU) there are rules that regulate the activities of public sector buyers. Contracts with a value above a certain threshold must be advertised: it is not an option for a buyer to source locally without inquiring widely for potential suppliers.

3.12 International sourcing introduces special additional factors. Historically, sourcing from abroad has been attractive primarily because of the opportunity for cost savings. Certain overseas countries have been strongly competitive because of cheap wage rates and easy access to abundant supplies of local raw materials. Countries nearer home have been at a price disadvantage as a result.

3.13 Another reason has been the quality revolution which was pioneered in the Far East, and especially in Japan. Often, Western purchasers have found that reliability, quality and even cost considerations favoured suppliers from such countries, despite apparent disadvantages arising from physical distance.

3.14 Finally, an important feature of some markets has been the rise in countertrade. Under a countertrade agreement, a company exporting to a foreign country may be 'requested' (ie required) to purchase materials from organisations in that country. Typically, these agreements have taken place with countries that suffer from lack of hard currency, including many countries in Eastern Europe. The main problem is that in some cases the goods offered in return for securing export sales suffer from quality defects that discourage potential trading partners.

4 Global aspects of supply chains

Offshoring

4.1 The term 'offshoring' refers to the relocation of business processes to a lower cost location, usually overseas. In recent years this has become a familiar practice – most readers will have had the experience of telephoning a large organisation and finding themselves talking to a call centre in, say, India. Although the term is particularly familiar in the context of services, some companies have also relocated their production facilities.

4.2 This practice is in essence a form of outsourcing but the overseas element gives rise to additional considerations.

4.3 In relation to production offshoring, there is an important issue relating to patent law. Companies will hesitate to offshore research and development work to countries where patent protection is weak, because of the danger that overseas workers could steal the ideas. Moreover, it is often difficult to find the required skill sets for difficult research and development work in regions with cheap labour. For these reasons, it is more common to find companies retaining R & D in the home country, and offshoring only the actual manufacturing.

4.4 Services offshoring has become possible through the growth in communications infrastructure. It is now common to find services such as call centres and data processing carried out in low-cost countries such as India, the Philippines and Eastern European countries.

4.5 Clearly a major attraction for companies in the West is the cost advantage that this policy offers. However, it is easy to exaggerate this. During 2005, an outsourcing consultancy (Ventoro LLC) carried out a major survey of organisations who have adopted offshoring, and found that cost savings actually achieved (approximately 19% on average) fell far short of what had been expected (40% or more). Even so, this is a significant saving.

4.6 Apart from the possible cost savings, supporters of offshoring point to the benefits of free trade, providing jobs to the poorer country and lower costs to the origin country. Though jobs may be lost in the origin country, the workers are (in principle) able to move to higher-value jobs in which their country has a comparative advantage.

4.7 Naturally, this last point is disputed by those workers in developed countries who have lost their jobs. And from the buyer's point of view there must also be a concern that the quality of the service provided may decline. Many large companies have met with hostility from customers who have received poor customer service and technical support from overseas centres. Often the complaints have focused on an inadequate level of skill in spoken English, together with the resentment that some people feel at the general principle of 'exporting jobs overseas'.

4.8 A further criticism of offshoring is that workers in less developed countries are subject to exploitation. Some critics even go so far as to say that the very reason why companies are adopting this approach is so that they can avoid the higher standards of worker protection that prevail in the West.

4.9 Offshoring also, arguably, increases the level of risk in the supply chain. It is more difficult for a buyer to exercise control over a service provider who is geographically distant.

Considerations when sourcing from another country

4.10 There are particular problems in dealing with suppliers abroad. Perhaps the most awkward issue to deal with is that of quality. As already mentioned, one reason for the increase in international sourcing has been the desire of Western firms to benefit from the quality advances pioneered in the Far East. However, not all overseas countries operate to the same quality levels as have become accepted in developed economies. The problem is made worse by the difficulty of making specifications unambiguous when a foreign language is involved. Absence of agreed international standards may also be a problem in some cases.

4.11 Price too is a more difficult issue than when dealing in home markets. The specific difficulties of dealing with foreign currencies come to the fore.

4.12 Delivery is likely to be slower and more uncertain. Political instability can wreck even the most tightly controlled schedules, but even without this complication sheer distance must be reckoned with. To compensate for longer lead times importers may order in large quantities, but this leads to high stock levels and associated costs.

4.13 Finally, the complications of international shipping procedures and documentation place additional burdens on purchasing staff. This is also the case in relation to payment methods.

Culture and communications

4.14 One of the more obvious problems in dealing with overseas suppliers is that they are not like 'us'! This remark is not intended in any racist or xenophobic sense. It is merely intended to make the obvious point that the residents of a particular country share a common culture and a common language, both of which influence their business dealings with each other. When dealing with overseas suppliers it is necessary to adjust to a different culture and language.

4.15 The difficulties here are both technical and behavioural. Technical difficulties concern the simple issue of understanding what is being offered and accepted, and what has eventually been agreed. Behavioural difficulties are related to how people interact with each other and form pleasant and rewarding business relations.

4.16 To deal first with the technical difficulty of communication, it is clearly vital that agreements once concluded are expressed in language that both parties understand. But before that stage is reached oral discussions will take place during which offers and commitments will be expressed that have a great influence on the course of negotiations. Buyers must make every effort to ensure that such discussions are unambiguous.

4.17 It is an essential element in a binding contract that the parties reach agreement. That element is absent if there is misunderstanding: one party believes he understands what the other has said, but in fact has not done so. Even leaving aside the legal niceties, it is clear that successful business relations are endangered if the two parties have different ideas as to what has been agreed.

4.18 Native speakers of English are in a fortunate position in that their first language is widely recognised as the standard language of international trade. However, that should not lead buyers to think that they can ignore communication difficulties. Even if negotiations are conducted in English, it is important to ensure that the supplier understands technical terms and idioms in the same way as the buyer.

4.19 An effort to acquire some understanding of the relevant foreign language can be a great help in this respect. It is also a major step in improving business relations. It is a positive sign that the buyer has made efforts to adapt to the supplier's position and will usually be welcomed even if the level of proficiency is not great.

4.20 This leads on naturally to the less technical and more behavioural problems of dealing with overseas suppliers. As in all negotiations, it is important to make a positive impression on one's business partners. This is more difficult in the case of overseas partners because of cultural differences.

4.21 Many of these differences have been described in the purchasing literature. For example, it is common to refer to Japanese patterns of business behaviour which can cause confusion to British and American buyers.

4.22 One instance of this is the much greater link between social and business relations in Japan; social communication forms a larger part of the negotiation process than is common in Britain or America. Buyers doing business in Japan should not assume that extensive entertaining by their hosts is an unimportant prelude to the main talks.

4.23 Another instance sometimes cited is the Japanese practice of avoiding a direct 'no', so as not to cause embarrassment to their guests. This can sometimes leave a British or American buyer believing that something is still up for debate, when the truth is that the supplier regards it as unacceptable.

4.24 Instances such as this could be multiplied by reference to other countries where business practices differ from those of Britain and America. However, the best practical measure is to benefit from the experience of others. Buyers doing business with overseas suppliers should brief themselves by discussing such points with colleagues who have previous experience. Some of Dobler and Burt's suggestions for dealing with overseas suppliers are listed in Table 8.2 below.

Table 8.2 *Suggestions for negotiating with overseas suppliers*

1.	Speak slowly and ask questions to check understanding.
2.	Print business cards in both English and the foreign language.
3.	Study the culture in advance.
4.	Be prepared for negotiations to be drawn out over a longer period than usual.
5.	Become familiar with local regulations, tax laws etc.
6.	Prepare in advance on technical issues, financing arrangements, cost and price analyses etc.
7.	If possible, ensure that the person recording the discussions is drawn from your team
8.	Arrange discussions so that the other team can 'win' their share of the issues.

Customs procedures, payment and legal issues

4.25 The documentation associated with international trade is extensive and often bewildering. This includes documents of title, shipping documents and many types of certificate relating to the goods (insurance, health, quality etc). Of course, not every one of these will apply to every transaction, but the buyer who sources from overseas must certainly reckon on a substantial increase in form-filling.

4.26 Goods imported will have to proceed through Customs. This leads to more paperwork, possible delays and a need to master fairly complex compliance procedures.

4.27 The supplier will also be concerned about the method of payment. The buyer would prefer payment to follow delivery and inspection; the supplier may prefer the reassurance of advance payment at least in respect of part of the total. Buyer and supplier must agree on whether open account trading is acceptable (as would be normal between businesses in the same country), or whether more elaborate payment mechanisms must be used. For example, it is common for suppliers to insist on a **letter of credit** issued by the buyer's bank to guarantee payment once the appropriate documents are received.

International transportation

4.28 The main types of transport mode used by industrial concerns are air freight, rail freight, road haulage, carriage by water (inland or overseas), and pipeline. In addition, certain specialised methods may be used for particular (usually small) consignments: an example is private courier services for delivery of small items where the demand is urgent.

4.29 The design of an overall transport strategy must take account of the particular features and benefits of all of these possibilities. In practice, it is likely that a combination of some or all will be used.

4.30 The prices charged by a haulier (whether by road, air, rail or sea) will depend on a number of factors such as the value of the product, the costs incurred by the haulier, the level of competition in the market and a number of less direct factors such as the extent of government regulation.

Incoterms

4.31 When buying from abroad, a purchaser may find himself involved in up to four separate contracts: the actual purchase contract, a contract of carriage, a contract of insurance, and a contract of finance (perhaps involving a letter of credit). The buyer must be able to cope with all of these, despite the language differences that may exist.

4.32 The communication difficulties involved in international trade have long been recognised as a problem. In particular, the interpretation of certain commonly used technical terms is of key importance to both buyers and suppliers, and must be absolutely free from ambiguity. A step in this direction was taken in 1936 when the International Chamber of Trade (nowadays the International Chamber of Commerce) published the first edition of *Incoterms*.

4.33 This publication, which has been updated frequently, sets out agreed explanations of many of the terms used in international trade to define obligations of seller and buyer. The incoterms were fully revised in line with developments in commercial practice, and republished in 2010. The current revision is effective from 1 January 2011. Many incoterms capture principles that have been used for centuries in international trade. Different interpretations had become possible, which are now standardised by incoterms.

4.34 Buyers and suppliers may contract with each other on whatever terms they think most suitable. They are not obliged to use incoterms. However, by doing so they remove many of the ambiguities that could otherwise be introduced into their agreement. If the agreement specifically refers to an incoterm, both parties understand immediately what their rights and obligations are in that respect. There is minimal danger of subsequent misunderstanding or dispute.

4.35 Parties may negotiate to determine which type of incoterm agreement is most suitable. In doing so the buyer should observe the need to develop a good business relationship on a long-term basis.

5 Supply chains in action

Differences in supply chains

5.1 Given the large number of different industry sectors, it is useful to consider the differences that may arise in the supply chain of an organisation. This is particularly of interest in connection with the means by which organisations sell their products. A useful distinction is between organisations that supply consumer products and those that sell industrial products.

5.2 The differences in the supply chains of such organisations are illustrated in Figure 8.5.

Figure 8.5 *Consumer and industrial supply chains*

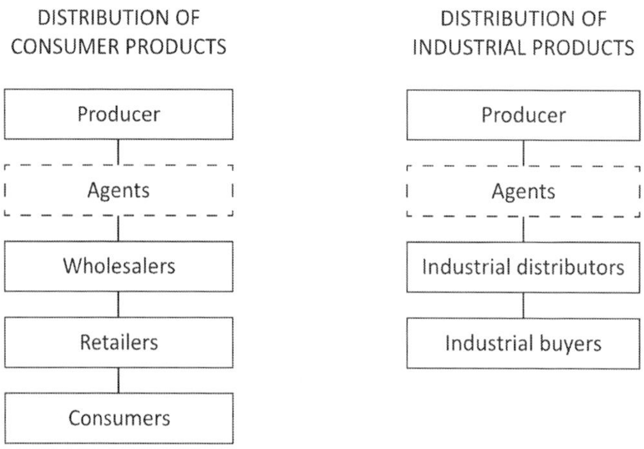

5.3 The use of agents depends very much on normal practice within the industry sector, as indicated by the dotted lines in Figure 8.5.

5.4 Figure 8.5 illustrated the downstream distribution of a producer's goods to the eventual customers. We might equally illustrate the upstream supply chain: see Figure 8.6.

Figure 8.6 *Example of an upstream supply chain*

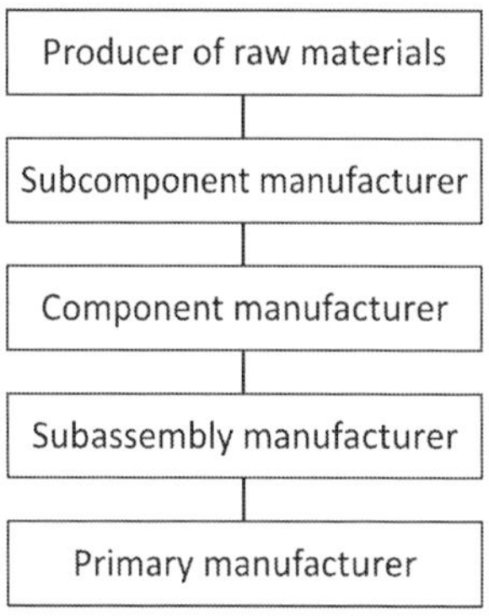

5.5 In a retail environment, the supply chain looks very different. See Figure 8.7, which is due to Baily *et al* in *Purchasing Principles and Management*.

Figure 8.7 *Supply chains in retailing*

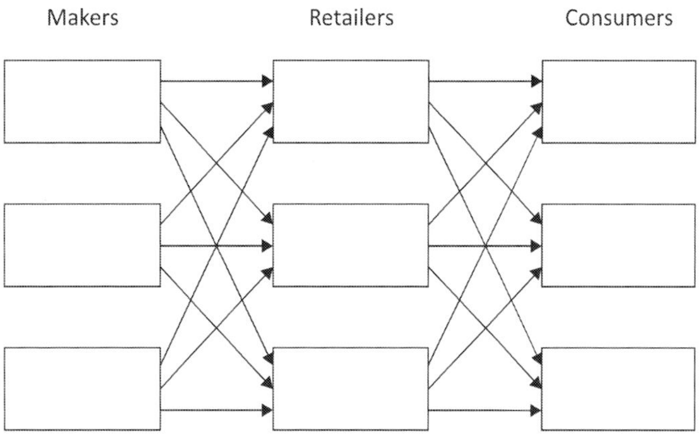

Chapter summary

- A supply chain links organisations (sometimes numerous) in delivering products or services to eventual consumers. Most organisations in the chain are both suppliers and customers of others.
- It is also possible to see relationships within a single organisation as forming a supply chain.
- To reduce the number of direct suppliers, an organisation may adopt a tiering system. Relations with first-tier suppliers will be very close and strategic.
- The concept of a supply chain leads on to the idea of supply chain management. It is not enough for a buyer to control his immediate suppliers; he must seek to improve efficiency and eliminate waste all along the chain.
- Increasing globalisation has had important consequences for both marketing and purchasing departments. For buyers, international or global sourcing is now common.
- A number of cultural, communications, logistical and documentation issues arise when sourcing from abroad.
- The large number of different industries gives rise to significant differences in supply chains for different organisations.

Self-test questions

Numbers in brackets refer to the paragraphs where you can check your answers.

1 Distinguish between customers and consumers. (1.6–1.8)

2 Explain what is meant by the internal supply chain. (1.14)

3 Why might an OEM adopt a policy of supplier tiering? (2.9)

4 List required characteristics of a first-tier supplier. (2.11)

5 What are the benefits of supply chain management? (2.28)

6 What arguments have been advanced against globalisation of commerce? (3.7)

7 What are the advantages of purchasing from overseas? (3.10ff)

8 What is meant by 'offshoring'? (4.1)

9 What are incoterms and how do they assist buyers sourcing from overseas? (4.31ff)

Subject Index